W9-DEH-942

LearnTCI Access Code

8261-0001-VWY2-TPR7-JBBS-HWR2

Social Studies Alive!®
Our Community and Beyond

T 56544

Chief Executive Officer: Bert Bower
Chief Operating Officer: Amy Larson
Director of Product Development: Liz Russell
Managing Editor: Laura Alavosus
Editorial Project Manager: Lara Fox
Project Editor: John Bergez
Editorial Associates: Anna Embree, Sarah Sudano
Production Manager: Lynn Sanchez
Design Manager: Jeff Kelly
Graphic Designer: James Whitehead
Photo Edit Manager: Margee Robinson
Photo Editor: Elaine Soares
Art Editor: Sarah Wildfang
Audio Manager: Katy Haun

TCi™ Teachers' Curriculum Institute
PO Box 50996
Palo Alto, CA 94303

Customer Service: 800-497-6138
www.teachtci.com

ISBN 978-1-58371-826-1
1 2 3 4 5 6 7 8 9 10 WC 15 14 13 12 11 10 09

Program Director
Bert Bower

Program Consultant
Vicki LaBoskey, Ph.D., Professor of
Education, Mills College, Oakland,
California

Student Edition Writers
Laura M. Alavosus
John Bergez
Diane Silver

Curriculum Developers
Kelly Shafsky

Reading Specialist
Barbara Schubert, Ph.D., Reading
Specialist, Saint Mary's College,
Moraga, California

Teacher and Content Consultants
Judy Brodigan, Elementary Social Studies
Supervisor, Lewisville Independent
School District, Texas

Lynn Casey, Teacher, Husmann
Elementary School, Crystal Lake, Illinois

Ann Dawson, Educational Consultant,
Intermediate Curriculum Specialist,
Gahanna, Ohio

Debra Elsen, Teacher, Manchester
Elementary, Manchester, Maryland

Candetta Holdren, Teacher, Linlee
Elementary, Lexington, Kentucky

Shirley Jacobs, Library Media Specialist,
Irving Elementary School, Bloomington,
Illinois

Elizabeth McKenna, Teacher, St. Thomas
Aquinas Catholic School, Diocese of
Orlando, Florida

Mitch Pascal, Social Studies Specialist,
Arlington County Schools, Arlington,
Virginia

Becky Suthers, Retired Teacher, Stephen
F. Austin Elementary, Weatherford, Texas

Lisa West, Instructional Specialist,
Language Arts/Social Studies, Landis
Elementary School, Houston, Texas

Tiffany Wilson, Teacher, Corbell
Elementary, Frisco, Texas

Beth Yankee, Teacher, The Woodward
School for Technology and Research,
Kalamazoo, Michigan

Literature Consultant
Regina M. Rees, Ph.D., Assistant
Professor, Beeghly College of Education,
Youngstown State University,
Youngstown, Ohio

Music Specialist
Beth Yankee, Teacher, The Woodward
School for Technology and Research,
Kalamazoo, Michigan

Maps
Mapping Specialists, Ltd. Madison,
Wisconsin

Table of Contents

Chapter 1
Where in the World Is Our Community?

Travel from outer space back to Earth. Learn geography terms along the way. Discover how to find any place on a map.

Reading Further: Explorers Find New Lands

Chapter 2
Where in the United States Is Our Community?

Find your community on a map of the United States. Read about famous places around the country. Find them on a map, too.

Reading Further: Eagles, Flags, and Midnight Parades

Chapter 3
What Is the Geography of Our Community?

Discover how to describe the geography of a place. Explore features of land and water. Learn about climate and natural resources. Read about the geography of three places in the United States.

Reading Further: Telling Stories with Maps

Maps

Where in the World Is Our Community?

Picture yourself as an astronaut on a NASA space shuttle. If you looked at the planet Earth from space, what would you see? Clouds? Land? Water? What would you need to know to find your landing site on Earth?

To answer these questions, you need to know some **geography**. Geography is the study of Earth—its land, water, air, and people. In this chapter, you will learn about some geography terms, such as *hemispheres, continents, countries,* and *states*. These terms will help you use maps to find any place on Earth.

Planet Earth

1.1 Our Community Is on Planet Earth

Remember that you are an astronaut in space. Earth looks big outside your window. How would you describe the shape of Earth? What else has this shape? A ball? Another word for an object with this shape is **sphere**. If you cut a sphere in half, you get two hemispheres. **Hemisphere** means half of a sphere.

Imagine a line around the middle of Earth, like a belt that goes around your waist. There is a line like this on maps of Earth. We call it the **equator**. It divides Earth into the Northern Hemisphere and the Southern Hemisphere.

You can also divide a sphere from top to bottom. Imagine a line that starts at the top of Earth and runs down one side of Earth to the bottom. There is a special line like this on maps of Earth. It passes through the city of Greenwich, in England. We call this line the **prime meridian**. It divides Earth into the Western Hemisphere and the Eastern Hemisphere.

Look at the maps on this page. Find the equator and the prime meridian. How many hemispheres do you see?

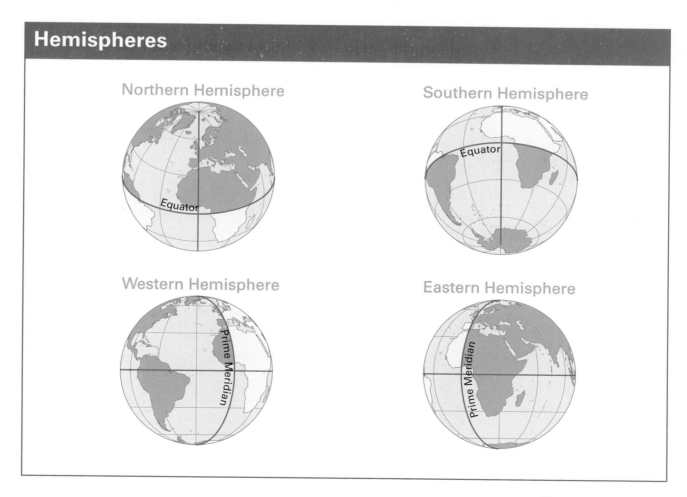

Hemispheres

Northern Hemisphere

Southern Hemisphere

Western Hemisphere

Eastern Hemisphere

1.2 Our Community Is on a Continent

From space, you can see that most of Earth is covered with water. The largest bodies of water are called **oceans**.

There are four oceans on Earth. They are called the Pacific Ocean, the Atlantic Ocean, the Indian Ocean, and the Arctic Ocean. Look at the map to find the four oceans.

The four oceans wrap around large bodies of land. These areas of land are called **continents**.

There are seven continents on Earth. They are called Africa, Antarctica, Asia, Australia, Europe, North America, and South America.

Oceans and Continents

ARCTIC OCEAN

EUROPE

ASIA

NORTH AMERICA

ATLANTIC OCEAN

PACIFIC OCEAN

AFRICA

EQUATOR

PACIFIC OCEAN

SOUTH AMERICA

INDIAN OCEAN

AUSTRALIA

ATLANTIC OCEAN

PRIME MERIDIAN

N

W E

S

0   1,500   3,000 miles

0   3,000 kilometers

160°W 140°W 120°W 100°W 80°W 60°W 40°W 20°W 0° 20°E 40°E 60°E 80°E 100°E 120°E 140°E 160°E

80°N
60°N
40°N
20°N
0°
20°S
40°S
60°S
80°S

ANTARCTICA

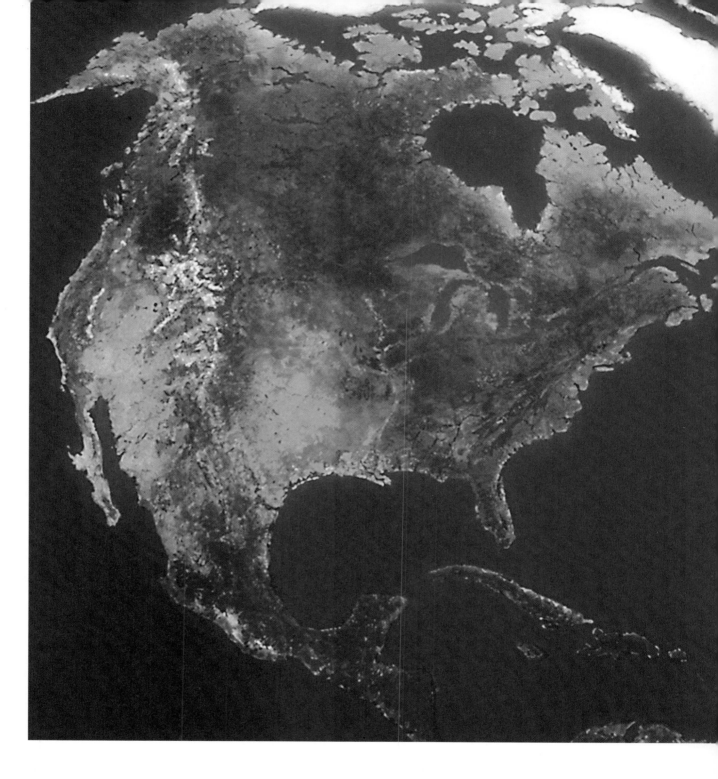

Asia is the largest continent. Australia is the smallest. Look at the map to the left to find each of the seven continents.

On which continent do you live? Do you live near an ocean?

What continent is this?

1.3 Our Community Is in a Country

Now you are steering the space shuttle toward your continent. Can you land just anywhere? What part of the continent do you need to find?

Most continents have many **countries**. A country is an area of land that has its own government.

Some countries are very large. For example, find Canada and the United States on the map to the right. They are quite large.

Other countries are much smaller. For example, find Cuba and El Salvador. They are small countries.

Where on this continent do you need to go?

8

From space, you can't see **borders**. A border is
the line where one place, such as a country, ends and
another begins. On a map, you can see lines drawn
around each country to show its borders. Sometimes
mountains, rivers, and oceans help to make borders.
At other times, countries have to agree on where their
borders will be.

How many countries can you find on the map
below? Where is your country on the map?

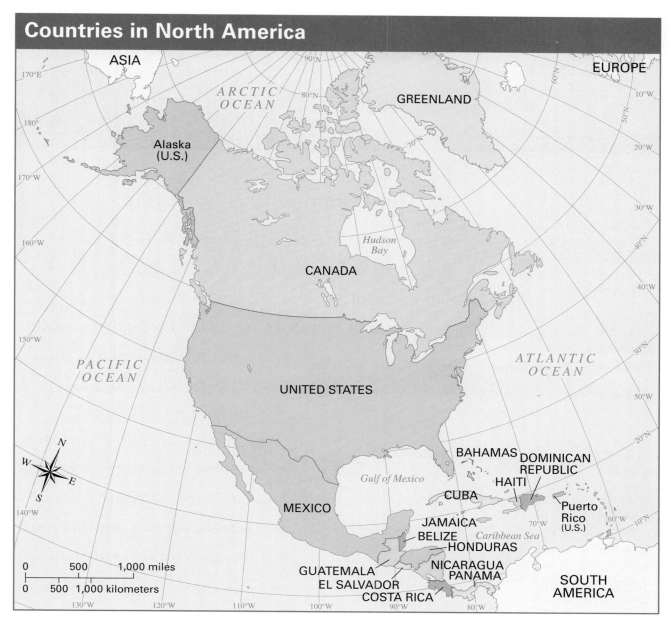

Countries in North America

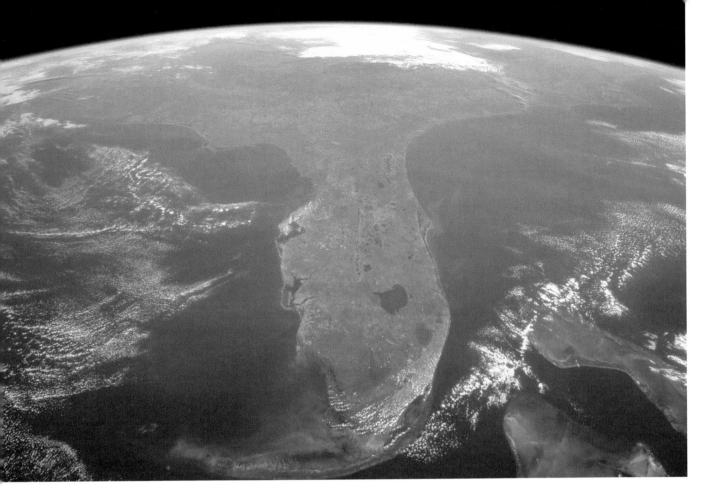

What part of the
United States are
you headed for?

1.4 Our Community Is in a State

The space shuttle is zooming toward the United States. It is a big country. How will you find the landing spot?

Most large countries are divided into many smaller parts. In the United States, these smaller parts are called **states**.

Your landing spot is in a certain state. Of course, you can't see the borders of states from space. Luckily, you have a map. You can see the map on this page. It shows part of the United States. Can you figure out which state the shuttle is flying to?

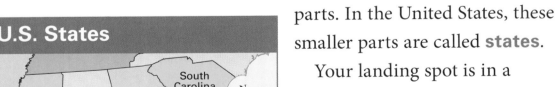

Some U.S. States

10

1.5 Finding Communities in a State

NASA confirms that you are headed for the state of Florida. States are made up of many **communities**. Communities are places where people live, work, and play. Some are called **cities**. They have lots of buildings and people. Other communities are smaller. We call them **towns**.

The community with your landing spot is somewhere in Florida. Can you find it?

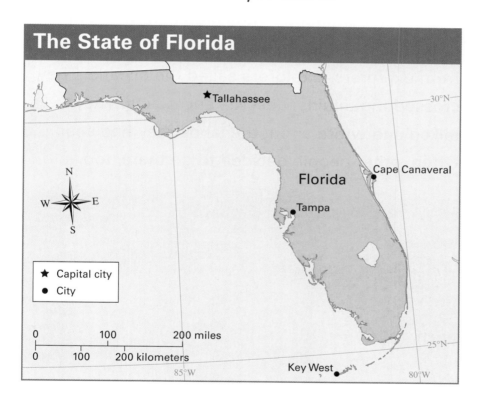

The State of Florida

Summary

In this chapter, you learned how to tell where places are on Earth. The names of hemispheres, continents, countries, and states all help us to say where a place is. Where on Earth do *you* live?

Explorers Find New Lands

Many of our towns and cities were started by people from Europe. But at one time, North America wasn't even on their maps. They didn't know our continent was here. How did they learn about it?

Five hundred years ago, people knew much less about Earth than you do. They didn't know Earth had seven continents. They didn't know it had four oceans. People slowly learned these things from explorers. Explorers sailed the oceans. They crossed mountains, deserts, and plains. They talked and wrote about the lands they had seen. Often, other people decided to go there, too.

This map of the world was made in the 1400s. How is it different from world maps today?

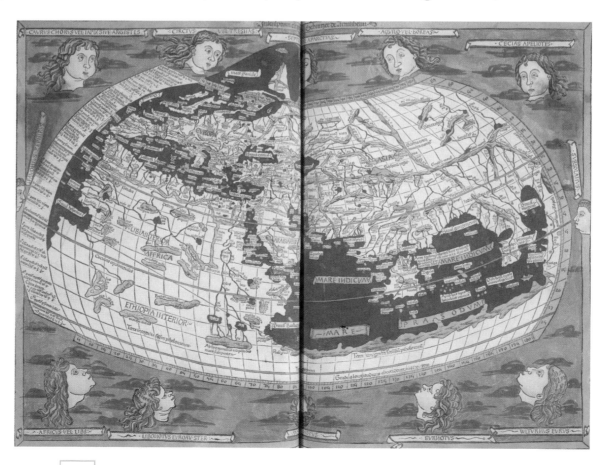

Explorers Come to North America

It was October 1492. Three small ships tossed in the waves of the Atlantic Ocean. Many of the sailors on the ships were angry and frightened. They were trying to do something no one had done before. They were trying to sail west from Europe all the way to Asia. But they had been at sea for ten long weeks, and still there was no sign of land. The men were afraid they might never see their homes again.

The sailors' leader was an explorer named Christopher Columbus. He told them to be patient. He was sure Asia wasn't far away.

Then, on October 12, a sailor shouted, "Land!" Ahead lay a green island. That morning, Columbus led his men ashore. He was very excited. He always said later that he had reached Asia. But he had really come to North America.

For Europeans, this was a new land. But millions of people already lived here. They were the American Indians. Now their land had been found by Europeans.

Christopher Columbus

Columbus started his trip in Spain. Where did he end up?

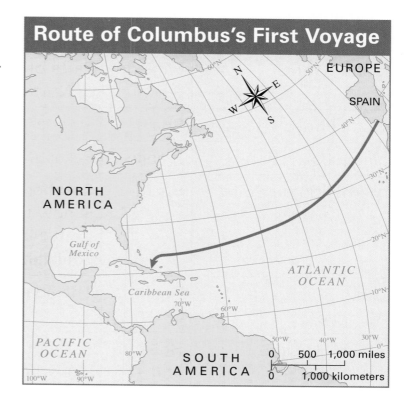

Route of Columbus's First Voyage

American Indians lived in North America long before Europeans arrived.

Soon more explorers came. Some explored the west coast of North America. One of them was Juan Rodríguez Cabrillo (keh-BREE-yoh). He worked for Spain. In 1542, he sailed north from Mexico. He was the first European to see California.

Cabrillo never made it home. He died after he was hurt in a fight with some American Indians. But his men did get back. They told what they had seen. Later, Spain sent people to live in California.

People also sailed to the east coast of North America. Some came looking for riches like fur. Others came to stay and start new communities.

Some European Explorers of North America			
Explorer	**Country**	**Places Explored**	**Years**
Christopher Columbus	Spain	Islands in the Caribbean Sea	1492–1504
John Cabot	England	Parts of the east coast of North America	1497–1498
Juan Ponce de León	Spain	Florida	1513–1521
Jacques Cartier	France	Parts of eastern Canada	1534–1542
Hernando de Soto	Spain	Southern parts of what is now the United States, from North Carolina to Louisiana	1539–1542
Juan Rodríguez Cabrillo	Spain	The coast of California	1542
Henry Hudson	Holland and England	Parts of eastern Canada and what is now New York State	1607–1611
Robert de la Salle	France	The Mississippi River	1679–1682

Crossing North America

In 1776, people on the east coast formed a new country. We call it the United States. Americans soon began pushing west. But they knew very little about the vast land ahead of them.

In 1804, President Thomas Jefferson sent a team of men to explore this land. Two friends led the team. They were Meriwether Lewis and William Clark.

The men started their trip in the middle of the continent. They paddled up rivers. They crossed grassy plains. They climbed snow-topped mountains. American Indians helped to guide and feed them along the way.

The team made it all the way to the Pacific Ocean and back. Americans were thrilled. They cheered Lewis and Clark as heroes. Now people knew much more about "the West." In the years to come, many Americans would decide that the West was a fine place to live.

The Granger Collection, New York

Lewis and Clark kept notebooks during their trip. They used words and pictures to tell what they saw.

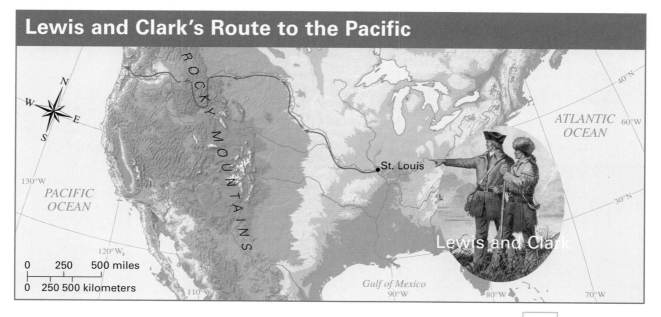

Lewis and Clark's Route to the Pacific

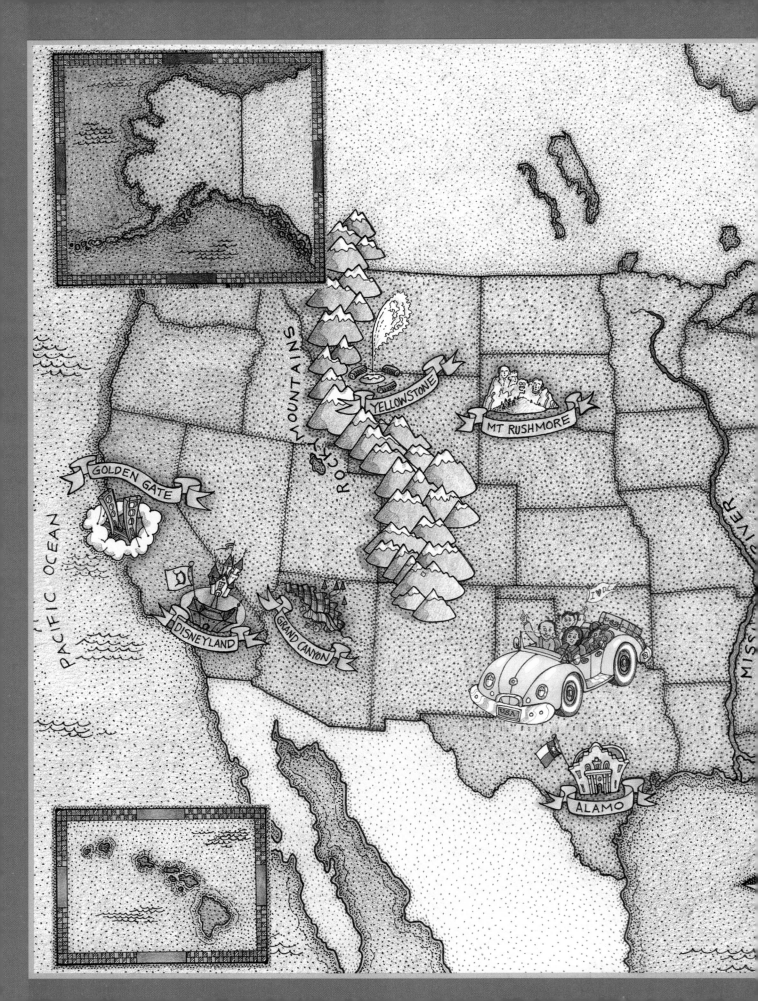

Where in the United States Is Our Community?

Your community is the place where you live. What is the name of the town or city where you live?

We use maps when we travel from one place to another. Maps show directions. North, south, east, and west are the **cardinal directions**.

In this chapter, you will find your community on a map of the United States. You'll read about some famous places and find them on a map, too.

HERSHEY

STATUE OF LIBERTY

WHITE HOUSE

ATLANTIC OCEAN

EVERGLADES

2.1 The 50 States

When you write your address, first you write the name of your street. Then you write the name of your community. Then you write the name of your state. These place names tell people exactly where you live.

There are 50 states in the United States. Each state has lots of communities in it. Which state do you live in?

The 50 States

2.2 The Statue of Liberty

Look at this picture. It shows a very big statue. This famous statue welcomes people to the United States. It stands for freedom. It is called the Statue of Liberty.

Many people visit the Statue of Liberty every year. It is on a small island in New York City. This huge city is in the state of New York. New York is near the Atlantic Ocean.

Do you live near New York City?

2.3 The Everglades

Have you ever seen an alligator? Would you like to meet a crocodile? You can in a famous place called the Everglades.

The Everglades are warm and wet. Lots of birds, snakes, crocodiles, and alligators live there. People visit the Everglades to camp, to see wildlife, and to fish.

The Everglades are in the state of Florida. Florida is north and east of the Gulf of Mexico.

Do you live north or south of the Everglades?

2.4 Mount Rushmore

Look at the faces carved into this mountain. Do you know who they are?

Mount Rushmore shows the faces of four famous U.S. presidents. The faces are 60 feet high. It took 14 years to carve them.

Mount Rushmore is in the state of South Dakota. South Dakota is west of the Mississippi River. It is east of the Rocky Mountains.

Do you live east or west of the Rocky Mountains?

2.5 The Grand Canyon

Why do you think we call the place shown below the Grand Canyon? A **canyon** is a deep, narrow valley with steep sides. Grand means large. The Grand Canyon is certainly large! It's 277 miles long and 1 mile deep.

Many people visit the Grand Canyon just to see it. Some hike or ride mules down to the bottom. A river runs along the bottom of the canyon.

The Grand Canyon is in the state of Arizona. Arizona is east of the Pacific Ocean. It is west of the Mississippi River. Do you live near a river?

2.6 The Golden Gate Bridge

The Golden Gate Bridge crosses the entrance to San Francisco Bay. The Pacific Ocean is west of the bridge.

The bridge opened in 1937. It had the tallest towers of any bridge in the world.

The city of San Francisco is at the south end of the bridge. People cross the bridge to get to other parts of the state of California.

Do you live near a famous bridge?

Summary

There are many interesting places in the United States. Maps help us to find states and the places within them.

Think about the places you have just read about. Which ones would you like to visit?

Eagles, Flags, and Midnight Parades

Your community is one of many in the country. Some are east of the Rocky Mountains. Some are west. But people all over the United States feel connected. What makes us feel part of one big community?

"Let's hurry," Marisa said to her friend Jacob. She ran up the steps of her school. Marisa was excited. Her school was helping to plan her town's Fourth of July celebration. Her class had chosen Jacob and Marisa to go to the planning meeting.

Marisa's town is called Gatlinburg. It is in the state of Tennessee. People there love to make the Fourth of July a special day.

A Fourth of July parade in 1923

A Fourth of July parade in 1999

The meeting was in the school library. Marisa and Jacob took their seats. Then Ms. Lundstrom stood up. She was the school's principal.

"Welcome!" she said. "As you know, the Fourth of July is a very important day. On that day in 1776, the Declaration of Independence was approved. This great document said that our country would be free. It would no longer be ruled by Great Britain. So July fourth is the birthday of the United States. How can our town make this year's Fourth of July the best ever? Let's hear your ideas."

A boy named Justin spoke first. "We've got to have the Midnight Parade," he said. "That way we have the very first parade of the day. It's a big tradition here in Gatlinburg." A **tradition** is something that people do together year after year.

The Granger Collection, New York

Thomas Jefferson wrote the Declaration of Independence. People still read his words today.

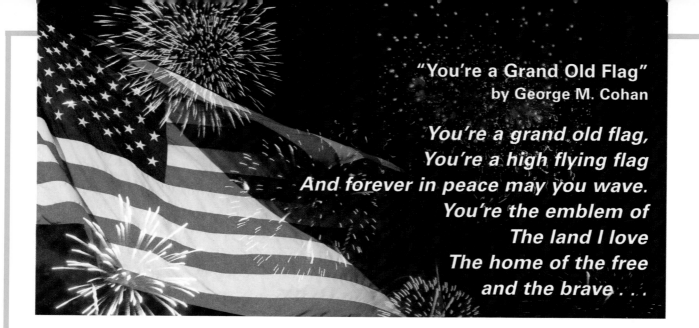

"You're a Grand Old Flag"
by George M. Cohan

You're a grand old flag,
You're a high flying flag
And forever in peace may you wave.
You're the emblem of
The land I love
The home of the free
and the brave . . .

People have been singing this song about the flag for more than 100 years. *Emblem* means symbol. In the song, what is the flag a symbol of?

"But how can we make the parade special?" Ms. Lundstrom asked.

"We could have giant balloons," Marisa said.

"Maybe some could be shaped like bald eagles," Jacob added.

Everyone liked that idea. The bald eagle is the national bird. It is a **symbol** of courage and freedom. A symbol is something that stands for an idea.

Then Tina spoke. "A band should lead the parade," she said. "It should play patriotic songs."

"The band should play 'The Star-Spangled Banner,'" Marisa said. "It's the national anthem."

"We learned some other good songs," Justin said. "I like 'You're a Grand Old Flag' and the 'Liberty Bell March.'"

"Wonderful!" Mrs. Lundstrom said. "These songs tell about American symbols. The flag stands for our strength and for everything that makes us one country. The Liberty Bell stands for freedom."

"I saw the Liberty Bell once," Marisa said. "It's in the city of Philadelphia. People rang it in 1776. They were going to read the Declaration of Independence out loud. They wanted everyone to come and hear it being read."

"That gives me an idea," Tina said. "Let's set up a booth to tell about our history. Someone can read the Declaration. And we can show a copy of the Constitution. Then people can see the words that gave us our government."

"And we could have pictures of the U.S. Capitol building," Jacob said. "That's where people write our laws."

Other students added more ideas. Marisa smiled. The Fourth of July plan was sounding better and better. She could see herself marching down the street at midnight. She could even hear the band playing!

The Liberty Bell has had a crack in it since the 1800s. No one has rung it since then.

What Is the Geography of Our Community?

What do you think of when you hear the word *geography*? Maybe you think of maps and globes. If so, you're right. In this book, you've used geography skills to help you find places on a map.

But geography isn't just about where places are. It's also about what different places are like. In this chapter, you'll read about the **physical geography** of three places in the United States. You'll learn what makes these places different from one another.

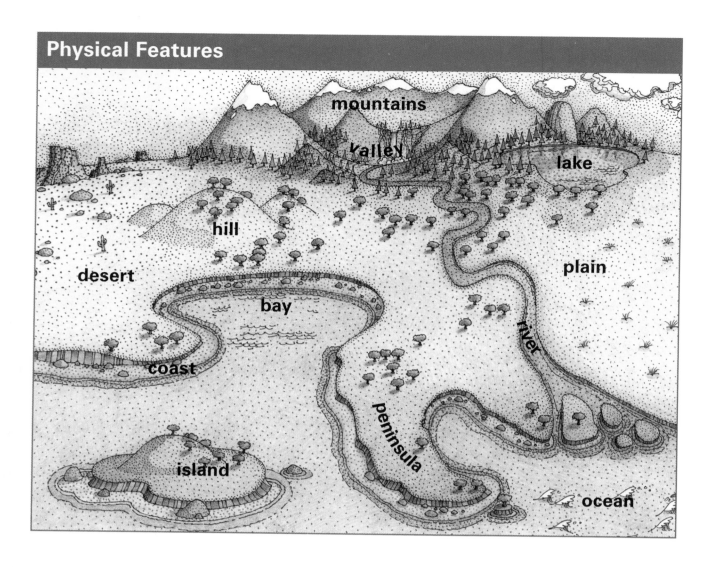

Physical Features

mountains

valley

lake

hill

plain

desert

bay

river

coast

peninsula

island

ocean

3.1 What Is Geography?

If you went for a bus ride near your community, what would you see? Would you see tall mountains? Flat plains? Would you see a lake or a river? These are all **physical features** of Earth's surface. Physical features are made by nature, not by people. They are part of the physical geography of the area where you live.

The geography of a place includes other things, too. For instance, **climate** is a part of physical geography. Climate means what the weather in a place is like, measured over time.

Of course, the weather can change from day to day. But different places often have different patterns of weather. Some places get lots of rain. Others hardly ever see a cloud. Some places are icy cold in winter and boiling hot in summer. Others have mild weather almost all year round. What is the climate like where you live?

People use many things from nature in their daily lives. These things are called **natural resources**. People use wood from trees to build houses. They use land and water to grow food. These resources are also part of physical geography. What are some of the natural resources near your community?

People use land and water to grow food.

How does climate affect what these people do for fun?

31

3.2 The Geography of Roseburg, Oregon

Geography has a lot to do with how we live. To see why this is so, let's look at three cities. We'll start with Roseburg, Oregon.

Oregon is in the Northwest **region** of the United States. A region is an area with certain features in common. The Northwest has lots of mountains, trees, and rivers.

People in Roseburg know all about these physical features. Roseburg is in a valley of the Cascade Mountains. Tall trees cover the mountains. A big river runs through the city.

A view of Roseburg, Oregon

The climate in Roseburg is gentle and mild. It rarely gets very cold or very hot. Winters are cool and rainy. Summers are warm and dry.

Roseburg's climate helps plants and trees grow. Forests are the most important natural resource in Roseburg. People work in lumber mills. (Lumber is wood that has been cut from trees.) The workers cut down trees and send the lumber to other places.

Lumber mills have been in Roseburg for many years. Some people make sure that more trees are planted to replace those that are cut down. Why do you think they do this?

Tall forests grow in the mild climate of the Northwest.

A worker at a lumber mill

A view of Las
Cruces, New Mexico

3.3 The Geography of Las Cruces, New Mexico

The city of Las Cruces (lahs-CROO-says) is in New Mexico. This state is in the Southwest region of the United States. This is a region of sandy deserts and rugged mountains.

The geography of Las Cruces has three important physical features. First, Las Cruces is in the middle of a desert. Second, there are mountains nearby. Third, the city was built next to a river. The river is called the Rio Grande. This name means "great river" in Spanish.

Las Cruces has a desert climate. The weather is usually hot and dry. There is very little rain. In the summer, it is very hot. Temperatures often climb over 100 degrees.

Can you guess what the most important natural resource in Las Cruces is? It's water. Deserts have very little water. But people, animals, and plants all need water to live. The people in Las Cruces try to use their water wisely. They are careful not to waste it.

The desert around Las Cruces is very dry.

3.4 The Geography of Gloucester, Massachusetts

The city of Gloucester (GLAWS-ter) is in Massachusetts. This state is in the Northeast region of the United States. The Atlantic Ocean is to the east of this region.

The ocean is the most important physical feature near Gloucester. In fact, the city has ocean water on three sides.

People in Gloucester need lots of different clothes. The weather there changes from season to season. Summers are warm and sunny. Winters are cold and snowy. Spring and fall are cool and rainy.

Fishing boats in Gloucester, Massachusetts

The weather around Gloucester even changes from day to day. People in this part of the country have a saying. They say, "If you don't like the weather, wait five minutes and it will change."

Fish and other seafood are the most important natural resources in Gloucester. Many people fish for a living. They spend days at sea on fishing boats. Then they sell the fish they have caught. Other people dig for clams or trap lobsters.

Summary

In this chapter, you read about three cities. The cities have different kinds of land and water around them. They have different climates. They have different resources. All these things are part of their geography.

What is the geography like where you live? Suppose you moved to a place with a very different geography. How might your life change?

Telling Stories with Maps

Your community may be near a lake or a desert. The land may be flat or hilly. You might have natural resources nearby, such as trees or fish. Maps can show all these things. But how do maps get made?

Hi. My name is Belinda. I tell stories about places. But I don't use words. Instead, I use maps. I'm a cartographer. That's a fancy name for a person who makes maps.

I can tell many kinds of stories with my maps. How do I decide what story to tell? The answer depends on two things: the purpose of the map and who is going to be reading it.

A cartographer at work

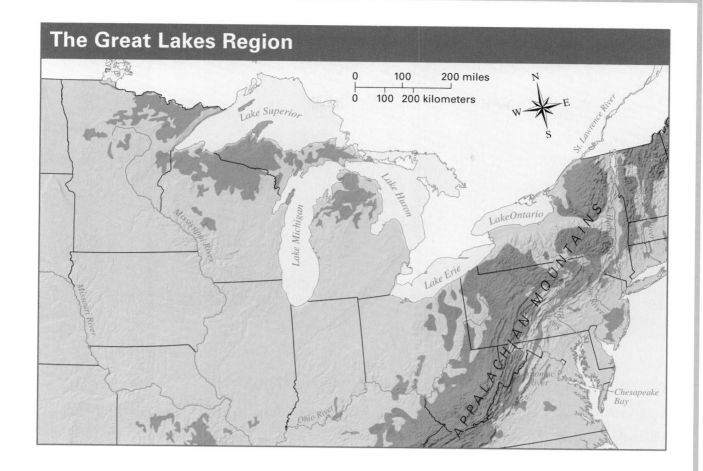

The Great Lakes Region

Let's say that the map's purpose is to show the main physical features of the Great Lakes region of the United States. Students like you will study the map to learn about these features.

My job is to create a map that shows you these things. I need to show features like rivers, lakes, and mountains. But I won't show lots of other things, like roads and cities. They would be important on a different kind of map, but not this one. On this map, I want people to look just at physical features.

So where do I start? I have to be sure that I put all the important features on my map. And I have to put them in the correct locations. My first step is to gather all that information.

A map showing physical features

39

An aerial photo of the Great Lakes region

How I Gather Information

Where do I get my information? I use other maps. I also use books.

Sometimes I use aerial photographs. These are photos taken from a plane. I can put several of these photographs together to see a large area.

I can also look at photographs taken from space. The space shuttle carries cameras into space. So do satellites. Satellites are spacecraft that go around Earth. Photographs taken from space are very useful for showing Earth's physical features.

Next I have to choose a type of map to draw on. Such a map is called a base map. This time, I will use a base map that shows the outline of the entire United States. The base map will also show state borders. These lines will help you see where different features are.

How I Put Information on a Map

The mainland of the United States is about 3,000 miles wide. I have to show that huge area in a space that will fit in a book like this one. I also have to squeeze in Alaska and Hawaii. So I need to figure out how many miles each inch of my map will stand for. Then I draw a scale on the map. The scale will help you measure the distances between places. I also draw a compass rose so you can tell directions.

Next I choose colors for the map. I use colors to help you see things quickly and easily. For instance, I might use shades of green for most land areas. But I might use brown for mountains and other high places.

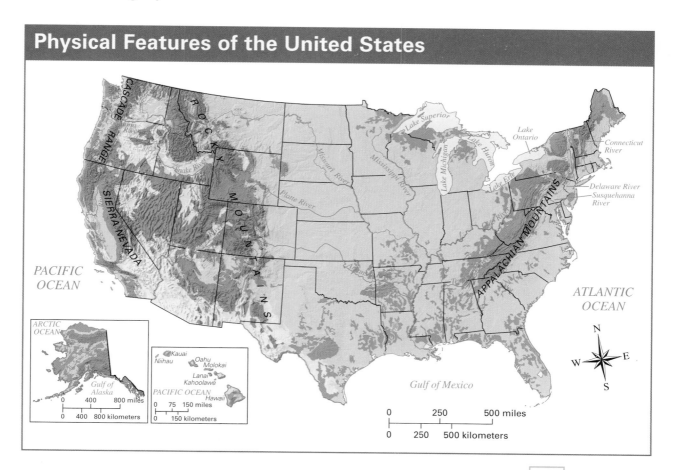

Physical Features of the United States

How I Help You Locate Features

I'm not done yet. I want you to be able to tell the location of places on the map. One way to do this is to draw a grid on the map. A grid is made up of squares in columns and rows, like the squares in a game of tic-tac-toe.

I give each column a letter and each row a number. Now we can name every square on the grid. For example, find the column labeled D in the grid to the left. Now move a finger straight down this column to the second row. You have found the square D2.

We can use grids like this one to say exactly where a place is. Look at the map below. Can you find Lake Erie? It's in square E2.

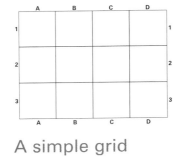

A simple grid

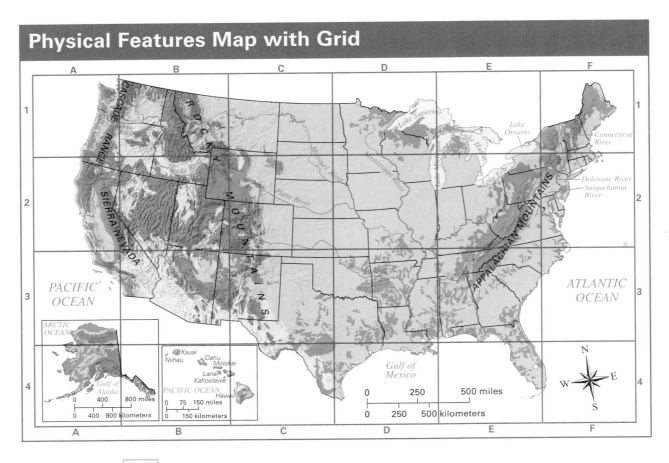

Physical Features Map with Grid

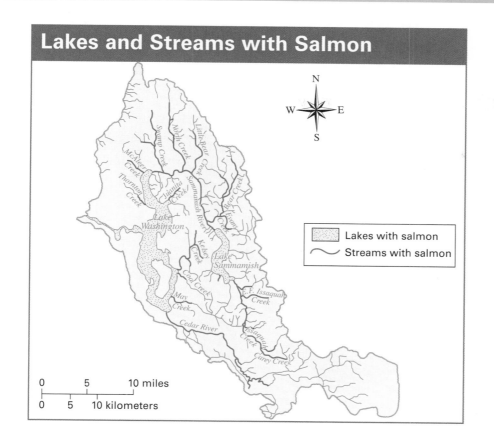

Lakes and Streams with Salmon

Lakes with salmon
Streams with salmon

The map above shows where salmon are found in a small part of the state of Washington.

How I Make a Special-purpose Map

Sometimes maps tell a story about a single topic. This kind of map is called a **special-purpose map**.

Here's an example. In the Northwest, fish called salmon are an important resource. People catch salmon to sell and to eat. But in some places, salmon are dying out. Maps can help us keep track of the salmon so we can protect this resource.

I can make a special-purpose map to show where the salmon are. First I gather my facts. I find out which lakes and streams have salmon. Then I use symbols to show this information on a map. I put a key on the map to tell what the symbols mean. (A key is also called a *legend*.)

I love telling stories with maps. And I love knowing that my maps help people learn more about their world.

43

How Do People Become Part of Our Country?

People from many places live in the United States. But how did we all get here? American Indians have lived here for thousands of years. But most groups came much more recently.

Europeans began to come here about 500 years ago. Since then, people have come from all over the world.

When people move to another country to live, they are called **immigrants**. In this chapter, you'll learn about immigrants. You'll find out why and how people come here to live. And you'll explore how they become part of our country.

4.1 Why Immigrants Come to the United States

People come to the United States for many reasons. Sometimes they may need to get away from problems. There might be wars where they live. Or the laws might be unfair. Sometimes there are too many people in a place. Then there may not be enough jobs or food for everyone.

Once, a disease started to kill all the potato plants in the country of Ireland. Potatoes were an important food there. When the plants died, people began to starve. Many families left their homes and moved to the United States.

Immigrants from Ireland came to the United States on ships.

People don't move here just to escape problems. Often they simply want a chance for a better life.

That is one reason our country grew quickly in the 1800s. Many people came from Europe to get good jobs or to start farms. Then gold was discovered in California. People came rushing to the gold fields from all over the world. Only a few of them got rich. But many stayed anyway.

Can you think of some reasons why people might want to come to the United States today?

Thousands of people rushed to the gold fields in California.

47

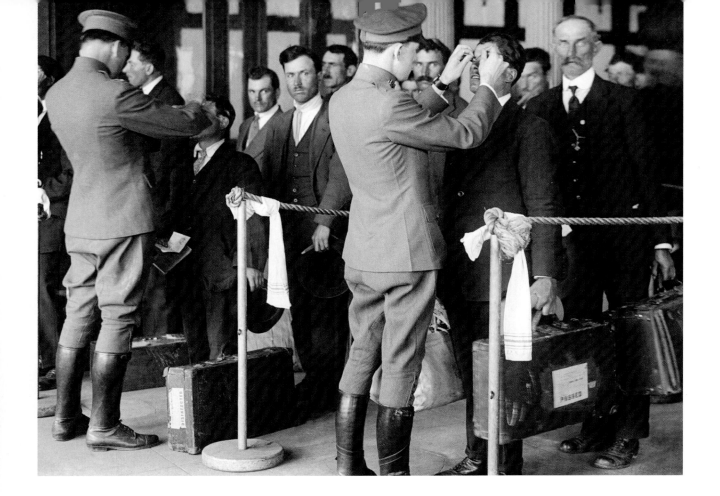

Immigrants had to show they were healthy. These immigrants had their eyes checked for disease.

4.2 How Immigrants Come to the United States

Getting to the United States is often very hard for immigrants. In the past, people came from Asia and Europe on crowded ships. They spent weeks crossing the ocean. People from the country of Mexico and other places sometimes walked hundreds of miles.

Things weren't easy after the trip was over, either. New immigrants were tested to see if they were healthy. If they were sick, they could be sent home.

Immigrants also had to answer a lot of questions. They had to say where they were going to stay. They had to show how they were going to make a living. Sometimes they didn't have good answers, and they were turned away. But millions were allowed to stay.

Getting to the United States can still be hard today. It can cost a lot, too. Sometimes whole families save money so just one person can immigrate. Often they hope the rest of the family can come later on.

Before coming to the United States, immigrants must get permission to stay here. They have to fill out lots of papers. They may have to stand in long lines to turn in the papers. Then they have to wait. Sometimes it takes years to get permission.

This man is hoping to get permission to enter the United States.

4.3 Life for Immigrants in the United States

Starting life in a new country can be hard. Sometimes people **discriminate** against immigrants. To discriminate means to treat people unfairly because they belong to a certain group. Also, some immigrants have to take jobs that no one else wants. These jobs can be dangerous. Often they don't pay much money. Many immigrants work long hours to earn the money they need.

Immigrants also find good things about life here. They may have more freedom than they had before. If they work hard, they may get better jobs. Then they and their children can have even better lives in the United States.

Immigrants often work long hours in difficult jobs.

Arnold Schwarzenegger

Isabel Allende

Some immigrants have become famous. Arnold Schwarzenegger (SHWART-sen-ay-ger) came here from Europe. He became a popular movie star. In 2003, he was elected to be governor of the state of California.

Isabel Allende (ay-YEN-day) is a famous writer. She came from South America. People all over the world love to read her books.

Summary

Immigrants come to the United States for many reasons. Some want to get away from problems such as war. Others hope for a good job or more freedom. Being an immigrant can be hard. But many people believe it is their best chance for a new and better life.

51

One Immigrant's Story

Each year, thousands of people choose to move to the United States. This is the story of one of those people. What was it like for a young girl to become part of our country?

When Carmen was ten, her family moved to the town of Reseda, California.

Carmen Gómez was born in Mexico. As a young girl, she lived in a small village called El Carmen. The United States seemed very far away. It was on the other side of deserts and mountains. Carmen never dreamed she might live there one day. Her home was in Mexico. But everything changed when Carmen was ten years old, as you'll find out.

Carmen's Old and New Homes

Reseda
California

Carmen's new home in California

UNITED STATES

Arizona

New Mexico

30°N

PACIFIC
OCEAN

25°N

N
W E
S

0   100   200 miles

0   100   200 kilometers

20°N

MEXICO

Carmen's old home in Mexico — El Carmen

115°W   110°W   105

Carmen's parents had six children. The family didn't have much money. Mr. Gómez, Carmen's father, traveled to the United States to work on other people's farms. When the work was done on one farm, he moved to another one.

People who move from place to place to get work are called **migrant workers**. Often they are not paid very much money. It was hard for Carmen's father to earn enough money for his big family.

Still, Carmen liked many things about her life. She had friends. She liked her school. "Every classroom had its own garden," she remembers. She liked that, too. She also liked being near her grandmother.

But Mr. Gómez was worried. He wanted to give his children an even better life. He needed to decide on the best way to do it.

Carmen's school

Carmen's home in Mexico

A Big Decision

Mr. Gómez faced a big decision. Should he go on working as a migrant worker? Or should he try to find a better job in the United States?

People have different ways of making big decisions. One way is to think about what will change if you make a certain choice. You can start with the good things that you think will happen. These good things are called benefits.

Mr. Gómez thought that moving to the United States would have many benefits. The main one was that he could get a better job. Then he could earn more money for his family.

He also thought his children would do well in the United States. They could go to public schools for free. In Mexico, parents had to pay to send their children to public schools.

Migrant workers get little pay for their hard work.

COSTS	BENEFITS
Transportation to United States	Better job
	More money for family!
Renting an apartment	No bills for school
Buying food	Good future for the children
Not seeing the family!!	

Mr. Gómez

Most decisions also have costs. For instance, Mr. Gómez would need money to move to the United States. Then he would need money for food and a place to live.

There was another kind of cost, too. Mr. Gómez would have to give up some things if he moved. He didn't have enough money to bring his family with him right away. That meant he would have to give up seeing his wife and children for a while. He would also have to give up the money he was making as a farmworker.

Mr. Gómez thought about all the benefits and costs. He tried to decide which ones were the most important. Then he made up his mind. He said goodbye to his family and began the long trip to California.

This old postcard shows the town of Reseda. It was very different from El Carmen.

Starting a New Life

When Carmen was ten, her family came back together. Her father had been working and saving money. He asked Mrs. Gómez and the children to come live with him in California.

Carmen was glad to be with her father again. "But I missed my school and my grandmother," she says. She was a little worried, too. She didn't know what life would be like for her now.

Carmen had felt at home in El Carmen. Reseda was a much larger place. Her family knew only one person. "We slept in the friend's garage until my dad could rent an apartment big enough for us," she remembers.

At first, it was hard to make friends. Carmen didn't speak English. It was hard for her to talk to classmates. She was glad that her neighbors were Mexican. They understood. They became like family to her.

Helping Other Immigrants

As time passed, Carmen learned to enjoy her new life. Learning English was hard, but she was a good student, and she loved to read. Every week she checked out books in English from the library. She also watched TV shows. The shows made her laugh, and they gave her practice with English. They also helped her understand American life.

Today, Carmen is a teacher in California. Many of her students are immigrants. They come from many countries. Like Carmen, most of them did not speak English when they moved here. She remembers how hard that was, so she helps them learn the language.

Carmen is proud to help her students get used to their new country. "Look," she tells them. "I came from Mexico. I slept in a garage. I had very little. Now, my brothers and sisters and I have gone to college. This country is my home now. Soon you will feel at home, too."

Carmen likes to teach her students Mexican dances. This picture shows her dressed up for dancing.

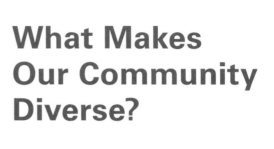

What Makes Our Community Diverse?

Our country is a very **diverse** place. Diverse means made up of different groups of people.

The people in a group have things in common. They may speak the same language. They may eat the same kinds of foods. They may celebrate the same holidays. They may play the same games. They may wear the same clothes or live in the same kinds of homes.

These things are all part of a group's **culture**. A culture is a way of life shared by a group of people. In this chapter, you'll explore some of the things that different cultures bring to our communities.

5.1 Our Community Shares Different Foods

Food is an important part of any culture. When people move to a new place, they often keep making the foods they are used to. Our communities have people from many cultures, so we also have many kinds of foods.

Many popular foods come from Europe. Do you like gingerbread? Europeans have made it for hundreds of years. Spaghetti comes from the Italian culture. Bagels come from the Jewish culture in Europe.

Have you ever tasted borscht? It is a soup made from beets. Borscht comes from the Russian culture. How about a gyro (YEE-roh)? A gyro is a sandwich made with roasted lamb and pita bread. It comes from the Greek culture.

This Italian woman is cooking spaghetti.

Asian Americans also have brought their foods to the United States. Do you like Japanese sushi? Or Chinese chow mein (chow-MAYN)? What about pho? Pho is a soup of noodles and meat. It comes from the country of Vietnam. Have you ever had tandoori chicken? This spicy dish comes from India.

Many popular foods come from Latino cultures. These are the cultures of Mexico, Central America, and South America. For instance, you may like tacos and tamales (tuh-MAH-leez). They come from the Mexican culture.

African Americans share other foods. Hush puppies are made of fried cornmeal. Hoppin' john is a stew of pork, rice, and black-eyed peas.

What are some of the foods that people eat where you live? What cultures do these foods come from?

Chopsticks come from Asian culture.

Many people like to eat foods that come from African American culture.

61

Some stores sell newspapers in many languages.

5.2 Our Community Shares Different Languages

Most people in the United States speak English. But many of us also use other languages.

Millions of Americans come from Latino families. They may speak Spanish in their homes and with friends.

In fact, you probably speak a little Spanish, even if you don't know it! That's because we get many English words from Spanish. Two of these words are *guitar* and *mosquito*. There are many more. The names of many places also come from Spanish. *Florida* is one. This name comes from the Spanish word meaning flowers. *Nevada* is another Spanish name. It means "capped with snow." The state was named for the Sierra Nevada, a snowy mountain range.

English and Spanish both come from Europe. We get words from other European languages, too. Do you like cookies? The word *cookie* comes from Dutch. How about pretzels? *Pretzel* is a German word.

Long before Europeans came to our land, many American Indian groups lived here. They had hundreds of languages. People still speak some of these languages today, such as Navajo and Cherokee. Some English words and names come from these languages, too. *Skunk* is one example. Another is *Kentucky*.

What about where you live? What are some of the languages that you might hear in your community?

This neighborhood has street signs in two languages.

63

5.3 Our Community Shares Different Holidays

Do you like holidays? Holidays are more than days when we don't have to go to school or work. They are days when we honor important people and events.

Each culture has its own special days. Many of our holidays came to us from Europe. One is Valentine's Day. Europeans have celebrated this day for hundreds of years. The Irish brought us St. Patrick's Day.

Some days are important in more than one culture. For Japanese Americans, the fifth of May is Children's Day. For Mexican Americans, the same day is Cinco de Mayo (SINK-oh day MY-oh). This holiday honors a famous battle in Mexican history.

These dancers are part of a Cinco de Mayo celebration.

December is a month full of holidays. Kwanzaa honors the culture of African Americans. It lasts for a week. Jewish people celebrate the eight days of Hanukkah. People in many Christian cultures share the holiday of Christmas.

We celebrate the new year in different ways, too. For many of us, New Year's Day is the first day of January. For the Chinese, the new year starts on a different date each year. The Chinese New Year celebration goes on for 15 days.

What holidays do people celebrate where you live? Which ones do you share with your family and friends?

Many people like to light candles for Kwanzaa.

5.4 Our Community Shares Different Traditions

Every culture has its own traditions. Games and sports are part of these traditions. So are arts, such as music and dance. Other traditions can involve wearing certain clothes or doing other special things.

Many of our sports began as traditions in certain cultures. Do you like to play soccer? This sport came to us from Europe. So did golf, skiing, and ice-skating. Surfing came from the Hawaiian Islands.

We also enjoy gifts from many cultures in our music and other arts. Jazz, gospel music, and rock and roll all grew out of African American music. Salsa and tango come from Latino cultures. Japanese Americans share Kabuki, a kind of drama, or play.

Gospel music can be very lively.

Many cultures have their own dances. Do you know how to clog? Clogging was started in the United States by people from Ireland, Scotland, and other countries. How about the hula? This style of dancing comes to us from Hawaii.

What are some traditions that people share where you live? What are some favorite traditions in your family?

Our game of soccer comes from England.

Summary

Our communities are very diverse. You can see this in the foods we eat and in the languages we speak. You can see it in our holidays and in our traditions. Do our diverse cultures make your life more interesting? What do you think?

Many People, Many Ways of Life

Our land has been home to diverse cultures for thousands of years. Once, many groups of American Indians lived here. Each group had its own way of life. What were these cultures like, and how did they differ from each other?

Hello! Welcome to the Time Travel Express. This is a very special train. It travels through time as well as space!

Today the train will take us into the past to meet three groups of American Indians. We will see how they lived before large numbers of new settlers came to their lands.

Our first stop is the year 1600, in what is now the state of New Jersey. There we will meet a group called the Lenapes (luh-NAHP-ees). All aboard!

Lenapes preparing fish for cooking

The Lenapes

The Time Travel Express is taking us along the Delaware River. Later, this area will become part of the Northeast region of the United States. In 1600, it is home to the Lenape people.

We stop by a village near the river. Do you see the large houses with curved roofs? They are called longhouses. Several families can share one longhouse. The smaller round houses are called wigwams.

The Lenapes fish in the river. They get many of the other things they need in forests nearby. They use wood and bark from trees to build their houses. They also hunt deer and beavers. They use the skins from the animals to make clothes.

The Lenape women grow food in the gardens. They plant corn, beans, and squash. Many American Indians in this region grow these three crops. The crops are known as "the three sisters."

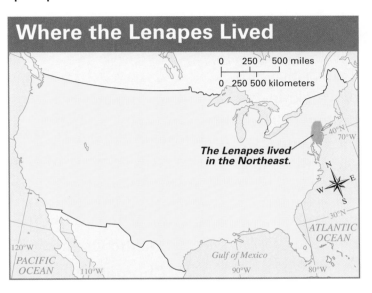

Where the Lenapes Lived

0   250   500 miles
0   250 500 kilometers

The Lenapes lived in the Northeast.

ATLANTIC OCEAN

120°W

PACIFIC OCEAN   110°W

Gulf of Mexico

90°W   80°W

40°N
70°W

30°N

A wigwam and a longhouse

The Chumash were skilled boat builders. The men used wood from trees to make their canoes.

The Chumash

Next, the Time Travel Express takes us to the Pacific Coast in the year 1750. One day, this place will be part of California. The city of Santa Barbara will grow up nearby.

We stop near a village that looks out on the Pacific Ocean. The village was built by the Chumash (CHOO-mash). Many Chumash live along the Pacific Coast. Some live on nearby islands.

About 2,000 people live in this village. The village has many dome-shaped houses. The Chumash cut branches from willow trees to make frames for their houses. Then they cover the frames with mats made from reeds, a type of plant.

Look out to sea. The men are out there in long, narrow boats called canoes. They are using long, sharp spears to hunt for seals, tuna, and whales.

Where the Chumash Lived

0 250 500 miles
0 250 500 kilometers

The Chumash lived near the Pacific Ocean.

40°N
70°W

N
W E
S

30°N

ATLANTIC OCEAN

120°W
PACIFIC OCEAN
110°W

Gulf of Mexico
90°W

80°W

On land, the men hunt deer and other animals. The women also help to gather food. They look for berries, wild plants, and acorns. The Chumash eat acorn soup or acorn cakes every day.

In Chumash groups, women can become leaders. A woman is the chief of this village. The chief tries to keep everyone safe. She also tries to make sure that no one goes hungry.

The Chumash wear little clothing. That is because the climate in this region is so mild. Sometimes the men wear just a belt to carry tools. The women wear skirts made of deerskin or woven from plants.

As we leave the village, watch for a cave nearby. Inside, colorful pictures cover the walls and ceilings. Religious leaders probably draw these pictures. It is their way of asking the gods to help the Chumash live a good life.

The Chumash made these colorful cave paintings.

Comanche women could put up a tepee in about 15 minutes.

The Comanches

Our last stop is in the year 1775. We are hundreds of miles to the east of the Pacific Ocean. Grassy plains stretch as far as we can see. One day, this place will be part of Texas. Right now, it is home to many groups of Comanches (kuh-MAN-cheez).

Over there, some women are setting up tepees. Tepees are a kind of tent. They are easy to set up and take down. This is important to the Comanches because they are always moving from one place to another.

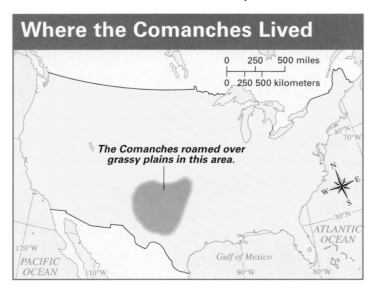

Where the Comanches Lived

The Comanches roamed over grassy plains in this area.

Why are the Comanches always moving? They move because they must follow the buffalo herds. The Comanches have built their way of life around the buffalo. Buffalo meat gives them food. The women make clothes and blankets from the skins. Even the tepees are made from buffalo skins.

The Comanches get other useful things from the buffalo, too. They make tools such as sewing needles from buffalo bones. They use the horns to make bowls and cups. They even use the buffalo stomach. It becomes a strong water bag.

The men and boys hunt the buffalo with bows and arrows. They make most of the bows out of wood, but sometimes they make bows from buffalo horns.

The Comanches used to hunt on foot. But then people from Europe brought horses to North America. The Comanches quickly became very skilled horseback riders. With horses, they can travel much farther to hunt buffalo. They also ride horses in battles against their enemies.

Our train is rolling again. We are returning to our starting place in our own time. I hope you have enjoyed our trip into the past!

Comanches were skilled hunters.

How Do People Improve Their Communities?

Our communities bring us many good things. They are full of diverse people and interesting places. But communities can have problems, too. When people see these problems, they can help solve them. Just one person can make a big difference.

In this chapter, you'll read about four people who set out to solve problems in their own communities. They each made their town or city a better place to live. Their work also helped people in many other places.

6.1 César Chávez Helps Farmworkers

César (SAY-zahr) Chávez came from a poor family. When he was still a teenager, he became a migrant farmworker to help his family.

Farmworkers had hard lives. They worked long hours for very little pay. Often workers got sick or hurt because they had to use unsafe chemicals and machines.

As a young man, César wanted to help the farmworkers. In 1962, he helped to start a new group. It became known as the United Farm Workers of America, or UFW. The UFW helped the workers ask for better pay and safer working conditions.

César Chávez (in the middle) made life better for farmworkers.

At that time, César lived in the town of Delano, California. There were farms all around the town. At first, the farm owners there refused to listen to the UFW. So César told all the workers to stop picking the crops. Stopping work in this way is called a **strike**. César hoped the strike would make the owners pay more attention to the workers.

The owners still didn't listen. César took another step. He asked people to stop buying what the farms sold. This is called a **boycott**.

It took five years, but many of the farm owners finally gave in. They agreed to pay the farmworkers more. The owners also promised that they would make the work safer.

César Chávez helped to make Delano a better place for farmworkers. He went on to help farmworkers in many other places around the country. César helped them get better pay and safer ways of working.

These people are marching to show their support for the UFW.

6.2 Ruby Bridges Helps African Americans

In 1960, Ruby Bridges was six years old. She was ready to start first grade. When she did, she would make history.

Ruby lived in New Orleans, Louisiana. At that time, black students and white students in New Orleans went to different schools. Ruby would be the first African American to go to the white school near her home.

Many white people were upset. They wanted black and white students to be kept apart. Still, Ruby's mother was hopeful. She thought the school was a good one. And she thought it was time that black and white children went to the same schools. But Ruby's father was worried. "We're just asking for trouble," he said.

Ruby's first day of school was frightening. Outside the school, crowds of angry people threw things at her. They yelled, "Blacks don't belong in our schools!" Ruby thought some of them might even hurt her.

Ruby Bridges made history when she was just six years old.

Inside the school, Ruby discovered she was the only student in her classroom. All the others had stayed home.

For months, Ruby was the only student in her class. Still, she kept coming to school. People started to see that she wasn't going away. One day, two white children came to school with her. Then more and more students came back to school.

Ruby made it easier for all children in New Orleans to go to good schools together. As an adult, Ruby helps people in other communities, too. She talks to children and adults about her experience and how we can still learn from it today.

Ruby helped to show people that black and white children could go to the same schools.

6.3 Lois Marie Gibbs Helps Make Her Community Safer

In 1978, Lois Marie Gibbs lived in Niagara Falls, New York. Lois had two children, Michael and Melissa. Michael became very sick. Lois wanted to know why.

There was an old **canal,** or waterway, near Michael's school. It was called Love Canal. Businesses had been dumping dangerous chemicals into the canal for years.

Love Canal flowed underneath the school playground. Lois thought the dirty canal was making her children sick.

Lois didn't know what to do. No one believed her fears about Love Canal.

Lois asked her neighbors about their health. It turned out that many of the children in the area were sick. Some scientists agreed that the canal could be the problem.

Lois decided to do something about it. She got all her neighbors together. Lois and her neighbors knew they needed help. They decided to tell everyone they could about their problem.

Lois Gibbs wanted to know why children near Love Canal were getting sick.

Lois and her neighbors made signs to carry. Then they followed the governor of New York around. People saw them on television.

Finally, the governor came to visit Love Canal. He agreed to help families move to a safer place. Later, President Jimmy Carter helped, too.

Lois Gibbs made a big difference in her community. Later, she helped people in other towns and cities. She showed them how to join together to make their communities safer places to live.

This school was closed because of the chemicals in Love Canal.

6.4 Judy Heumann Helps Disabled People

Judy Heumann (HEW-man) was born in 1947. When she was a baby, she got sick with polio. This disease hurt her legs. Judy would never be able to walk. She had to use a wheelchair to get around.

Judy Heumann started the group Disabled in Action.

Judy lived in Brooklyn, New York. On her first day of first grade, her mother brought her to school. The principal wouldn't let Judy in because she was in a wheelchair. A teacher came to Judy's house for a few hours each week instead.

When Judy was in fourth grade, she was finally allowed to go to school. There she met other **disabled** students. Disabled means not being able to do an everyday thing, like walk, talk, hear, or learn, in the same way that most people can. Judy learned that the other disabled students felt the same way she did. Her legs didn't work right, but she wanted to learn as much as any other student.

In college, Judy studied to be a teacher. At first, New York City wouldn't let her teach because she was in a wheelchair. Judy went to court to win the right to teach. She taught school for three years.

In 1970, Judy formed a group called Disabled in Action. She started the group to protect disabled people in New York from being treated unfairly. The group has grown a lot since then. Today it helps disabled people all across the country live better lives.

Thanks to Judy, disabled students like these are treated more fairly.

Summary

In this chapter, you met four special people. César Chávez, Ruby Bridges, Lois Marie Gibbs, and Judy Heumann all helped to improve their communities. They made other people's lives better. Their work helped people in many other places, too. What can you do to make your community a better place?

Helping a Community in Need

Sometimes problems are too big for a town or a city to solve by itself. In 2005, a flood put most of New Orleans under water. Homes and businesses were ruined. Thousands of people had no food or shelter. Who reached out to help?

The city of New Orleans sits on very low ground. Nearby there is a large lake.

Years ago, levees, or walls, were built to keep the lake's water from flooding the city. But in 2005, a huge storm struck New Orleans. Afterward, some of the levees broke. Water poured into the streets. It wrecked homes and trapped people and animals.

New Orleans needed help—and lots of it.

People being rescued from the flood in New Orleans

New Orleans

Helping People Survive

The storm that struck New Orleans was called Hurricane Katrina. Hurricanes are large storms with heavy rains and powerful winds. These storms can cause a lot of harm. So can other events in nature, such as earthquakes. We call these events **natural disasters**.

In a natural disaster, people need help. One group that gives help is the Red Cross. The Red Cross was started more than 100 years ago. It helps people in need around the world. The Red Cross does not try to make money. In fact, many of its workers are **volunteers**. This means they are not paid.

Hurricane Katrina struck a large area in the southern United States. Much of New Orleans was flooded, but other places were hit hard, too. Workers from the Red Cross rushed to the scene. They set up shelters for homeless people throughout the area. They brought drinking water and other supplies. They cooked hot meals. They helped many people survive the disaster.

A photograph of Hurricane Katrina taken from space

Red Cross volunteers passing out drinking water

85

Saving Animals

People were not the only ones needing help in New Orleans. Pets were in trouble, too. A group called the SPCA reached out to these pets.

SPCA stands for the Society for the Prevention of Cruelty to Animals. The SPCA has been helping animals in need for more than 100 years. Like the Red Cross, it does not try to make money.

The day before Katrina struck, the SPCA took 263 pets to Houston, Texas. It wanted to keep them out of danger. But the real work started after the flood. Dogs, cats, horses, and birds were stranded. Many of them died. Still, the SPCA rescued about 8,500 animals. It also worked to bring pets and their owners back together.

Dogs being rescued from the roof of a wrecked home in New Orleans

This girl is selling lemonade to raise money for people who were harmed by Hurricane Katrina.

Kids Helping Out

Melissa, Jenna, and Jackie Kantor live in the state of Maryland. After Katrina, they had an idea. They wanted to send backpacks to kids who were affected by the storm. The girls started Project Backpack. In two months, they collected about 50,000 backpacks! People from 40 states joined in to help them.

In Strongsville, Ohio, a Girl Scout troop helped, too. The scouts collected supplies for people who were hurt by Katrina. The scouts set up boxes in schools. Students put food, candles, blankets, and other items in the boxes. The scouts filled up about 25 vans with supplies.

Have you ever heard the saying "Every little bit helps"? That was very true after Katrina. Large groups reached out to help. So did many individuals. You can be sure that each little bit of help made a big difference.

How Are People Around the World Alike and Different?

You and your friends probably do many of the same things every day. What do you think children in other parts of the world do?

Some things are the same no matter where we live. Everyone eats and sleeps. Nearly all children play. In most places, children also go to school. But they don't all do these things in exactly the same way.

In this chapter, you will read about the lives of children in six different countries. As you read, think about how each child's day is like yours and how it is different.

7.1 Josie Lives in Canada

Josie lives in a small town in northern Canada. Josie's family is Inuit (IH-noo-wet). The Inuit people have lived in Canada for 3,000 years or more.

It is cold and snowy most of the year where Josie lives. Josie skis to school. Her best friend, Ivy, rides to school on a snowmobile. At school, they eat a hot breakfast.

Josie is learning to use a computer at school. Her other classes are reading, math, and history. Josie doesn't speak English. She speaks Inuktitut (ih-NOOK-teh-toot) with her family and friends.

On weekends, Josie's family sometimes goes ice fishing. They make holes in the ice and try to catch fish in the water below. Josie also likes to play in the snow with her dog, Max.

Ice fishing

One of Josie's favorite meals is caribou stew. Caribou are large deer that live in Josie's part of the world.

Josie's warmest boots are handmade from sealskin. Some of her blankets are made of sealskin, too. Josie, Ivy, and their friends use the blankets to play a blanket toss game. Lots of people play together. Several people hold the edges of the sealskin blanket. One person stands in the middle of the blanket, and the others toss him or her into the air. Josie and Ivy both love to bounce on the blanket.

Josie and her friends like to play blanket toss.

7.2 Luis Lives in Paraguay

Luis lives on a farm in the country of Paraguay. Paraguay is in South America.

Luis lives with his mother, father, and three brothers. He wakes up before sunrise every morning so he can help his father and brothers in the fields. There's always something to be done on the farm. Luis might plant seeds, hoe weeds, or pick crops.

Luis and his family often take a break to drink terere (teh-reh-REH). Terere is made in a cup with water and dried, crushed leaves. The cup is called a guampa (WAHM-pah).

The guampa is usually made from a cow's horn. Luis sips the drink through a metal straw. The straw has a strainer at one end to keep the leaves out.

Luis's father works hard in the fields.

Luis goes to school six afternoons a week. He and his brother Esteban (es-TAY-bahn) ride their family's horse to school. The school is several miles from their farm.

Luis's favorite part of school is playing with his friends. During breaks, they play soccer. They call the game fútbol (FOOT-bohl).

All of Luis's classes are in Spanish. Outside of class, Luis and his friends like to speak Guarani (gwahr-uh-NEE). Guarani is a language that people in Paraguay have spoken for hundreds of years. Luis likes the fact that people still speak Guarani today.

Luis and his brother with their horse

7.3 Kazuo Lives in Japan

Kazuo (kah-zoo-oh) lives in Kyoto (kyoh-toh). Kyoto is a large city in the country of Japan.

Each morning, Kazuo wakes up in the room he shares with his little brother. The small room has sliding doors made of paper. These doors are called shoji (shoh-gee). Kazuo and the rest of his family sleep on thick mattresses called futons. Each morning, they roll up their futons and blankets and put them in the closet.

For breakfast, Kazuo and his brother eat cereal. His parents eat rice and egg with chopsticks.

After breakfast, Kazuo's father hurries to catch the train to work. Kazuo's mother stays home to take care of his little brother.

The bedrooms in Kazuo's house have shoji and futons.

Meanwhile, Kazuo gets ready for school. First he gets his schoolbag. Then he goes to the front door to put on his shoes. Kazuo's family never wear shoes in the house.

Kazuo goes to school six days a week. He rides the bus with his friends. They all wear navy blue uniforms. Kazuo speaks Japanese with his friends, but in school he is studying English.

Kazuo and his friends practice a sport called kendo (ken-doh) in gym class. In kendo, the boys use bamboo sticks like swords. They put on face masks and gloves so they don't get hurt.

Kazuo likes to practice kendo.

7.4 Emma Lives in Hungary

Emma lives in a small city in the country of Hungary. Hungary is in central Europe.

Emma lives in an old house with her mother and two brothers. Every morning, Emma feeds the geese in the backyard. Then she eats breakfast before walking to school with her brothers, Viktor and Sandor (SHAN-dor).

Emma is in third grade. Her favorite class is music. She likes sewing class, too. All students in Hungary must learn a foreign language. Emma is learning French. She speaks Hungarian with her friends.

Emma's geese

Emma and her brothers are good at sports. Viktor plays soccer. Sandor is on the school's swim team. Their school has an indoor swimming pool. Emma practices gymnastics in school twice a week. Her favorite thing to do in gymnastics is the balance beam.

Emma has music lessons on Tuesday afternoons. She is learning to play the flute. Her mother thinks Emma plays beautiful music. But her brothers cover their ears when she plays. Someday, Emma wants to play the flute in an orchestra like her uncle Zoltan (ZOHL-tahn).

Emma likes to show her skill on the balance beam.

97

7.5 Paul Lives in Australia

Paul lives on a cattle ranch in the country of Australia. The cattle ranch is far from any city or town. Australians call this part of their country the outback. It's hot and dusty in the outback.

When Paul gets up in the morning, he puts on a T-shirt and jeans. Then he puts on tall leather boots. He wears a hat to keep the sun off his neck.

Paul eats eggs and snags for breakfast. Snags are sausages. After breakfast, Paul takes care of his horse, Scout. Later in the day, he'll ride out with his father to check on the cattle.

Paul and his two sisters go to school for an hour and a half a day. Actually, they don't go to school—school comes to them!

Paul and his family raise cattle on their ranch.

The school is called Schools of the Air. It comes to Paul and his sisters by radio. They use a two-way radio to listen to and talk to the teacher. Then they do homework.

Paul would rather be eating a sandwich than doing homework. Paul spreads a brown paste made from vegetables on bread or crackers. It's his favorite snack.

Once a week, Paul's family drives to the store in town. Sometimes they stop at another ranch to see if their friends need anything. Paul's friend, Gary, lives on this ranch. Paul and Gary like to play video games and ride their horses.

Would you like to go to school by radio?

99

7.6 Miriam Lives in Nigeria

Miriam lives in a town in the country of Nigeria. Nigeria is in Africa.

Miriam has 11 brothers and sisters. She helps look after the younger ones. She likes to use her doll to play-act stories for them.

Miriam likes school. She does well in math and geography. She also studies history and health.

Everyone speaks English at school. Miriam also speaks Hausa (HOW-seh). Hausa is one of hundreds of languages in Nigeria.

After school, Miriam watches television. Then she does her homework.

After homework, it's time for dinner. Food in Nigeria is very spicy. People often cook with hot peppers. Miriam eats a lot of rice, beans, corn, and yams. She also eats fruit every day. Mangoes are her favorite.

Miriam works hard in school.

Miriam also likes a soft drink that is made with ginger. Ginger is the spice used in gingerbread. Miriam likes the taste of ginger.

Miriam is learning to play the drums. "Talking drums" are an important part of juju music. Juju songs tell stories about local people and events. People play juju songs in the evenings. Miriam dances to the music with her friends.

These children are telling a story with juju music.

Summary

You have just read about children in six places around the world. In many ways, their lives are alike. For example, all of them go to school. In other ways, their lives are very different. What about you? How is your life like those of the children you read about? How is it different?

101

The Story of Mexico City

One reason that people around the world are different is that each place has its own past. How does the history of Mexico City help us to understand the people who live there today?

Carlos lives in Mexico City. His city is the biggest in Mexico. It is also Mexico's **capital**. A capital is the city where the government of a country meets.

Carlos's sister, Myra, has been learning about the city's past in school. Today she is taking Carlos on a tour to share what she has learned.

"We'll start at the main square," Myra says. "That's where the story of our city begins."

The main square in Mexico City

These carved snakes' heads were part of an Aztec temple.

The Aztecs

At the square, Myra tells Carlos how Mexico City grew.

"It all starts with the Aztecs," Myra says. "The first city on this spot was built by the Aztecs. The Aztecs were an American Indian group. They built a great capital city here in 1325. They called it Tenochtitlán (tay-noch-teet-LAHN). You can still see parts of Aztec buildings around the square today.

"The Aztecs told an interesting story about why they built their city here," Myra goes on. "The story says the Aztecs were looking for a place to settle. One of their gods told them to watch for an eagle sitting on a cactus. The eagle would be eating a snake."

"And the Aztecs found the eagle here?" Carlos asks.

"That's right," Myra says. "But in those days, this was just a muddy island in the middle of a lake."

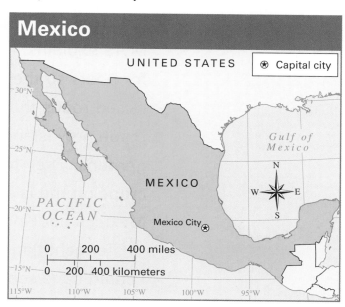

Mexico City is in the center of Mexico.

Diego Rivera, a Mexican artist, painted this picture of Tenochtitlán.

An Island City

"How could the Aztecs build a big city on an island in a lake?" Carlos asks.

"Well, they had to change their surroundings," Myra explains. "For instance, they built canals for boats so they could move around. They built raised roads that crossed the lake. They even made new islands that they used as floating gardens. They grew flowers, beans, and other crops on the islands. Beans are still a big part of Mexican cooking today."

"Tenochtitlán sounds neat," Carlos says. "I wish I could have seen it."

"We can go see a famous painting of what it might have looked like," Myra tells him. "It's in the National Palace, right here on the square."

The End of Tenochtitlán

"So what happened to Tenochtitlán?" asks Carlos.

"The Aztecs were very powerful," Myra answers. "And their city was large and beautiful. But in the 1500s, the Spanish came to Mexico looking for gold. They joined together with some American Indians who were the Aztecs' enemies. They fought the Aztecs and won. And that was the end of Tenochtitlán."

"Why?" asks Carlos.

"The Spanish tore down the Aztecs' great city," Myra says. "Then they built their own city in its place. They called it Mexico City. 'Mexico' comes from another name for the Aztecs."

Myra points to a large church. "The Spanish built that church long ago. An Aztec temple once stood there. The Spanish used stones from Aztec temples in many of their buildings. You can see still see old Aztec stones in some of these buildings today."

The Spanish built this church on the ruins of an Aztec temple.

A Mix of Cultures

"Spain ruled our country for 300 years," Myra goes on. "During this time, children of the Spanish and the Aztecs married. Their cultures mixed together. Meanwhile, the Spanish drained the lake around Mexico City. This let them build an even bigger city."

"But we aren't ruled by Spain any more," Carlos points out.

"That's right," Myra says. "In the 1800s, the people of Mexico rose up against Spain. After much fighting, they took control of their country. We still celebrate this event. A special bell hangs in the National Palace. The bell is rung once a year on September 15, the day before our Independence Day."

Carlos smiles. "So now the people were Mexicans like us."

Myra smiles too. "Yes, but the old cultures lived on. For instance, the people made buildings that mixed Spanish and Aztec styles. And we still speak Spanish today."

The National Palace is one of the old Spanish buildings in Mexico City.

Mexico City Today

"You see, Carlos," Myra says, "we are like these buildings. Most people in Mexico City come from both the American Indians and the Spanish. We have American Indian history in us, just like some of these buildings have Aztec stones."

"Mexico City has lots of brand-new buildings, too," Carlos says proudly.

"Oh, yes," Myra agrees. "Just look at the skyscrapers! Our city grew very fast in the 1900s. People came here to get jobs in factories and other businesses. Now our city is one of the biggest in the world."

"Hey, look!" Carlos points at a huge Mexican flag on a pole in the square. The flag shows an eagle standing on a cactus. A snake hangs from the eagle's beak.

"It's the old Aztec story!" Carlos says.

"That's right, Carlos," Myra answers. "The Aztecs are still with us, even in our flag."

Today Mexico City is one of the biggest cities in the world.

The Mexican flag

How Does Our Economy Work?

Have you ever been to a farmers market? Farmers markets are places where farmers bring crops to sell. A **market** is any place where buyers and sellers come together.

Buying and selling are big parts of our **economy**. An economy is made up of all the businesses in a place. Some businesses sell **goods**. Goods are items you buy, such as food or computers. Other businesses sell **services**. Services are tasks you pay people to do, such as cutting your hair.

How do sellers decide what prices to charge? Why do some goods and services cost more than others? In this chapter, you'll explore these questions.

Sellers want to get
as much money as
they can for their
goods.

8.1 We Buy and Sell Things

Suppose that you're a farmer. It's early summer. You have ripe green beans to sell.

As a farmer, you are a seller at the market. What price will you charge for your beans? You want to get as much money as you can. But you don't want to charge too much. Customers might not want to pay your price. They might go to another farmer who is selling green beans at a lower price.

Now suppose that you're a customer at the farmers market. You are now a buyer. You want to buy as many green beans as you can. You also want the best green beans. And you want to pay as little money as you can.

As a customer, you have choices. You can shop around to see who has the lowest price for green beans. But if lots of people want green beans, the farmers may want to see who will pay the most for them.

As you can see, markets bring together people who have different goals. Sellers want prices to be as high as possible. Buyers want prices to be as low as possible.

Markets also force people to compete with one another. Sellers compete for the same customers. And buyers sometimes compete to buy the same things.

Buyers can shop around for the lowest price.

8.2 Prices Change When Supply Is High and Demand Is Low

How do prices get set in a market? A big part of the answer is **supply** and **demand**.

Supply is the total amount of a good or service that is available to buy. At the farmers market, the supply of oranges is made up of all the oranges that are for sale. Demand is the total amount of a good or service the customers in the market will buy at a certain price.

Together, supply and demand affect prices. Here is an example. Suppose it's December. Farmers have brought lots of ripe oranges to the market. The supply of oranges is high.

What makes prices change?

Unfortunately for the farmers, their customers already have lots of oranges. They don't want more oranges. Demand for oranges is low.

Now the farmers have a problem. They have more oranges than customers want to buy. What do the farmers do?

One thing the farmers can do is lower their prices. If they make their prices low enough, customers might decide to buy some oranges after all. In fact, the farmers can compete with one another by making their prices lower and lower to attract buyers. So, when supply is high and demand is low, prices go down.

What do farmers do when they have more oranges than people want to buy?

8.3 Prices Change When Supply Is Low and Demand Is High

Can you guess what happens to prices when supply is low and demand is high? Suppose it is late July. The season for cherries is almost over. Few farmers have ripe cherries to sell. The supply of cherries is low. But many customers at the market want to buy cherries. The demand for cherries is high.

Now the customers have a problem. The demand for cherries is greater than the supply. What do the customers do?

Customers can compete with one another to get the cherries. They do this by being willing to pay more for the cherries than other customers. The farmers know this, so they raise their prices.

What do customers do when farmers don't have enough cherries to sell?

In other words, sellers know that buyers will pay more for something they want when there is less of it for sale. So, when demand is high and supply is low, prices go up.

Have you ever collected trading cards? If so, you may have seen supply and demand at work. Suppose you have a card that everyone else has. Your friends probably won't give you much for it. The supply of that card is high, and the demand for it is low. So, the price your friends will pay for the card is low.

What happens if you have a rare card? Your friends might trade two or three cards for it. That's because the supply of that card is low, while demand for it is high. Now the price of the card is high.

How much can you get for a trading card? It depends on supply and demand.

8.4 Changes in Supply or Demand

You've seen that supply and demand affect prices. So, what happens when supply or demand changes?

Suppose farmers in California have grown a huge crop of watermelons. There are more watermelons than anyone has seen in years. The supply of watermelons is way up. The farmers want to sell all their melons. What do they do? They lower their prices. The farmers know that customers will buy more watermelons if the price is lower.

Now suppose that there is freezing weather in Florida. The cold spoils half of the year's crop of oranges. The supply of oranges is way down. The farmers decide to raise their prices. Why? There aren't enough oranges for everyone who wants them. The farmers know that customers will pay more to get the oranges they want.

How can bad weather change the price of oranges?

What happens to prices when demand changes? Suppose that millions of sports fans see a famous athlete drinking apple juice on television. The fans decide that apple juice can make them strong. The demand for apple juice goes up. So does the price. Why? Sellers know they can charge more for something when lots of people want to buy it.

Here's one more example. The week before Halloween, lots of people want to buy pumpkins. The demand for pumpkins is higher, so prices go up. When Halloween is over, demand goes back down. So, farmers lower their prices so they can sell their pumpkins.

Why do pumpkins cost less after Halloween?

Summary

Supply and demand help to explain how markets work. High supply and low demand lead to low prices. Low supply and high demand lead to high prices. When either supply or demand changes, prices change, too.

117

Making Mail Faster

Businesses may sell goods, like fruits and vegetables. Or they may sell services, like hair cutting or mail delivery. How can demand lead to better services?

Suppose that your grandmother's birthday is tomorrow. You live in New York City. She lives in San Francisco, California. That's on the other side of the country! Can you get a birthday gift sent to her in time? Yes! You can pay a delivery company to ship your gift overnight.

Delivery of packages and other mail is a service you can buy. Mail delivery has gotten faster over time. Why? A big reason is that businesses compete for customers. One way to get more customers is to lower prices. Another way is to offer better goods or services.

Companies that deliver mail try to be fast. Why?

Fast Ships and Stagecoaches

Mail delivery used to be a lot slower than it is today. In the 1840s, mail could take six months to get from New York City to San Francisco. The mail was sent by ship. It had to go all the way around South America!

Six months was a long time to wait for mail. People wanted faster mail. The demand for better service grew.

Businesses tried to meet the demand. Some used faster ships. Then a man named John Butterfield tried something new. In 1858, his mail company started delivering mail across the country by land. The mail was carried on stagecoaches. The company said it could get mail from Missouri to California in just 24 days. But often it took months. People still wanted faster mail.

Mail Route in the 1840s

NORTH AMERICA
San Francisco
New York City
ATLANTIC OCEAN
40°N
20°N
0°
20°S
40°S
PACIFIC OCEAN
SOUTH AMERICA

• City

N
W   E
S

0   1,000 2,000 miles
0   2,000 kilometers

140°W   120°W   100°W   80°W   60°W   40°W

A Butterfield stagecoach

A Pony Express rider

The Pony Express

In 1860, one man saw a chance to make money by meeting the demand for faster mail. His name was William H. Russell. He had an idea for the fastest mail service yet. He wouldn't use ships. He wouldn't use stagecoaches. Instead, he would use fast horses and skilled riders to carry letters and other lightweight mail. Russell's new service became known as the Pony Express.

The Pony Express was designed for speed. A rider raced on horseback for about 10 to 15 miles. Then he changed horses and kept going. Each rider rode about 75 to 100 miles in a day. Then he tossed the mail he was carrying to a fresh rider. In this way, mail sped from Missouri to California in 10 days or less.

Faster and Faster

The Pony Express lasted just 18 months. It lost part of its job to an invention called the telegraph. The telegraph let people send messages to faraway places over electric wires. Then, in the 1860s, trains began to carry letters, packages, and other mail across the country.

In 1918, airplanes began carrying mail. Airmail was delivered by the U.S. Post Office Department. (Today we call it the Postal Service.) But new companies also started up to ship mail.

In 1977, one of these companies took a bold step. It promised to ship mail overnight. People loved the new service. Soon other companies offered overnight service, too.

As you can see, mail delivery has become a lot faster over time. Why? It all starts with demand. First buyers must be willing to pay for something. Then sellers will compete to give buyers what they want.

Speedy trains picked up bags of mail without even stopping.

Today people can buy a gift on the Internet and have it delivered the next day.

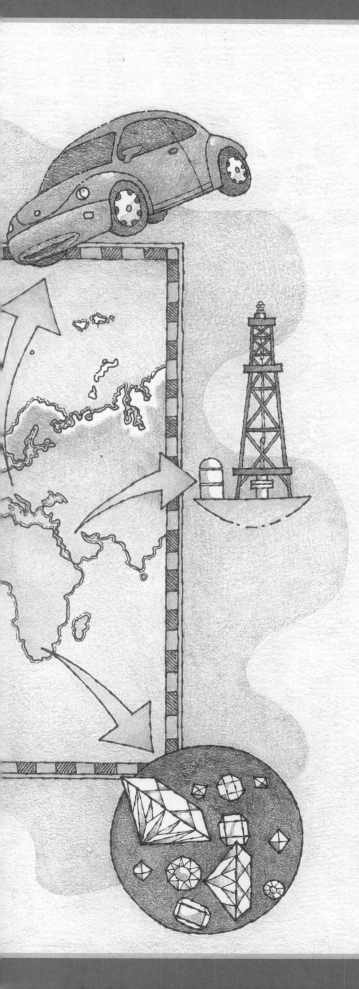

9

How Does Global Trade Affect Our Community?

It takes the whole world to get Jen to school in the morning.

Jen's clock radio wakes her up. The radio was made in Japan. Then Jen puts on her jeans and her favorite T-shirt. They were made in China. Jen's athletic shoes were made in Thailand.

As part of her breakfast, Jen eats a banana that came from Ecuador. Then she rides to school in a car designed in Germany. The gas in the car comes from oil found in Saudi Arabia.

You also use things each day that come from all over the world. In this chapter, you will learn how these things get to your community.

9.1 Countries Trade What They Have for What They Need

Have you ever traded things with your friends? Maybe you traded an apple for a banana at lunch. Or maybe you traded a toy for a game.

Trades work when people have things that other people want. This is true for people and for whole countries. For example, Ecuador grows lots of bananas. The United States grows some bananas, but it wants more. So, the United States buys bananas from Ecuador.

What does Ecuador need? Farmers in Ecuador need tractors. The United States has many factories that make tractors. So, Ecuador buys tractors from the United States.

A worker in Ecuador washes and weighs green bananas.

Ecuador sells bananas to the United States. The United States sells tractors to Ecuador. You could say that Ecuador trades its bananas for tractors. In the same way, the United States trades its tractors for bananas.

These kinds of trades go on all over the world. Together, they are called **global trade**. Today, global trade is bigger than ever before. One reason for this is that people have figured out better ways to move and store goods.

Many goods travel on container ships like this one.

9.2 Countries Trade Natural Resources

Countries have different natural resources. They trade resources they have for ones that they need or want.

Bananas are a good example. Banana plants grow best in hot, wet countries like Ecuador. That's why Ecuador has lots of bananas to sell. The United States buys most of its bananas from countries like Ecuador.

The United States has its own resources to sell. For example, wheat grows better in parts of the United States than it does in many other places. The United States sells lots of wheat to other countries that need it.

Another example is grapes. Grapes need warm weather to grow. During the summer, the United States produces lots of grapes. It doesn't need to buy grapes from other places. The United States even sells some of its summer grapes to other countries. But during the winter, the United States has to buy grapes from warmer countries such as Chile and Mexico. Global trade lets people in the United States enjoy grapes all year.

Many of our grapes come from places like this farm in Chile.

Oil, gold, and copper are also resources. The United States doesn't have enough of these resources to meet its needs. So it buys them from other countries. For example, Saudi Arabia has lots of oil. South Africa has many gold and diamond mines. Chile sells more copper than any other country in the world. The United States buys resources from all these countries. In return, it sells the countries things that they need.

An oil drill in Saudi Arabia

9.3 Countries Trade Goods That They Make

You have read why countries trade natural resources. Countries also trade **manufactured** goods. Something is manufactured if it is made with machines. Cars, watches, and shoes are all manufactured. Can you think of other examples?

Why do countries trade for goods that are made somewhere else? One reason is that some countries are known for their high-quality goods. Switzerland is famous for its fine watches. Many people like to buy cameras that are made in Japan. Germany designs some of the world's best cars. Some companies in the United States are known for making very good computers.

This car is sold in the United States, but it was designed in Germany.

Women sewing clothes in a factory in Asia

Other countries want these goods because of their quality. So, countries trade their own products to get them.

Some countries can make goods for less money than other countries can. For example, companies in many Asian countries can make clothes at a low cost. These companies pay their workers less money than companies in other places do. This lowers the price of the clothes they make.

Other countries buy these goods because of their low price. This is one reason your jeans, T-shirts, and athletic shoes may come from countries in Asia.

9.4 Benefits and Costs of Global Trade

Global trade brings both benefits and costs.

What are some of the benefits? Global trade allows people to buy things from all over the world. It allows people to enjoy quality goods. It also allows people to pay less for some goods. Without global trade, Jen might not have bananas for breakfast. Jen's dad might not have such a nice car. And Jen's athletic shoes might cost a lot more.

What are some of the costs? Global trade allows companies to move to countries where they can pay their workers less money. This takes jobs away from rich countries. It can also keep pay low for workers in poorer countries.

Workers making shoes in Thailand

Workers can lose jobs when companies move to countries where costs are lower.

Suppose a shoe company in the United States moves its factories to Thailand. What happens? The company saves money. But the American workers lose their jobs. And the workers in Thailand get low pay.

Also, global trade means that people don't always buy things made locally. So, local companies may lose business. Some may even have to shut down.

Summary

Global trade connects countries around the world. Countries trade what they have for what they want or need. They trade natural resources. They also trade goods that they make. Global trade brings benefits to many people. It allows people to buy quality goods and low-cost goods from other places. But global trade also has costs. Some countries may lose businesses and jobs to other countries. And in poorer countries, global trade may keep workers' pay low. So, is global trade good or bad? What do you think?

How Trade Is Changing Bangalore

Countries trade resources. They trade goods they make. Countries also trade services. This kind of trade can bring about big changes in a community. How is the global trade in services changing one city in India?

You're writing an e-mail to a friend. Suddenly, your e-mail stops working. You need help. You call the company that runs your e-mail service. A young man named Ravi (RAH-vee) answers the phone. He helps you fix your e-mail.

Ravi isn't in your town. He isn't even in the United States. He's talking to you from Bangalore (BANG-guh-lawr), India. Many U.S. companies have moved some of their work there. As a result, life is changing fast for people like Ravi.

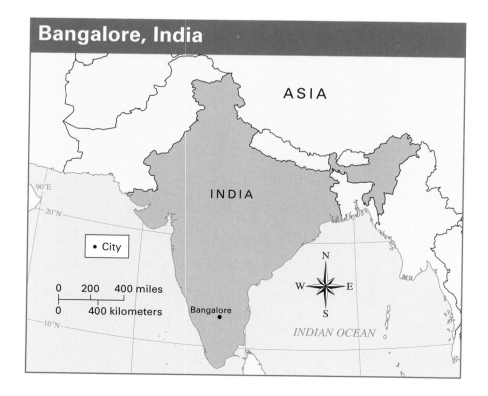

Bangalore, India

Why Companies Move Services to Bangalore

Ravi works in a call center. A call center is an office where people help customers who call in about a product. Many U.S. companies have moved their call centers to India. Why? The main reason is to save money. Companies don't have to pay workers as much money in India as they do in the United States.

But why do the companies choose Bangalore? One reason is that the workers speak English. This means they can talk to customers in the United States. Also, the city tries to make it easy for companies to move there. For example, it has a school that trains people to work with computers.

Today, Bangalore is one of India's fastest growing cities. There are lots of new jobs for people like Ravi. But there are also big changes in the way people live.

Many companies have moved their call centers to Bangalore.

Life is changing fast in Bangalore. Today the city is a mix of old and new.

How Ravi's Life Is Changing

A year ago, Ravi lived with his parents. Most young people in India stay with their families until they are married. They do not have enough money to live on their own. Then Ravi got his job at the call center. Now he earns enough money to take care of himself. He lives in a new apartment. It is one of thousands of new apartments being built in Bangalore.

Ravi is still trying to get used to the noise and smell of all the traffic in the city. When Ravi was little, Bangalore had about 3 million people. Today it has more than 6 million! About 5 million cars, trucks, and motorcycles creep through the crowded streets. And there are still wooden carts pulled by oxen, too. The carts add to the traffic jams.

Other parts of Ravi's life are changing, too. When Ravi was a boy, he spoke a language called Kannada (KAH-nuh-duh). He learned English to get his job. Now Ravi hears more and more people speaking English.

Ravi used to go shopping with his family in the markets in the old part of the city. Ravi still likes to touch and taste the fresh fruits and vegetables there. But mostly he goes to fancy stores and shopping malls now. Sometimes he eats at one of the new fast-food restaurants.

Ravi's parents worry about some of the changes they see. They are afraid of losing their old ways of life. "I still like the old ways," Ravi tells them. "But changes are sure to go on. We're part of a much bigger world now, and there is no going back again."

Bangalore still has its old street markets, but it also has fancy new shopping malls.

135

What Are the Public Services in Our Community?

As you have learned, services are tasks that people do for you. Businesses sell many services to people who want them. These are called **private services**. Towns and cities offer other services to everyone. These are called **public services**.

People can use public services for free or at a low cost. This is because **taxes** help to pay for these services. Taxes are money that people and businesses pay to a government. For example, families in most states pay a sales tax on many things they buy.

What are some public services? You'll find out in this chapter.

10.1 Police

All communities need to keep the peace. Providing this service is the job of the police.

Police keep the peace in several ways. They make sure that people obey laws. For example, police give tickets to drivers who don't stop at red lights. Police walk or ride through neighborhoods to make sure people are safe. They arrest people who steal or commit other crimes.

Police also help people in other ways. They direct traffic. They give directions to people who are lost. They help rescue people when floods, earthquakes, and other disasters happen.

Police make sure that people obey laws.

Police around the world are both alike and different.

Police around the world are alike in many ways. But they are also different. Some police ride in police cars. Others ride motorcycles. In some places, the police use bicycles. In other places, they ride horses. In Egypt, you might see police riding camels!

Have you ever heard of the Mounties? They are a famous police force in Canada. Their full name is the Royal Canadian Mounted Police. They are called the Mounted Police because they used to ride horses. Today, most Mounties travel by car, by helicopter, or by snowmobile.

How do the police help people where you live? What would your town or city be like without its police?

10.2 Health Care

Have you ever needed help from a nurse or a doctor? Nurses and doctors are health care workers. Health care workers take care of people who get hurt or sick. They also try to keep people from getting sick in the first place.

In the United States, people can get some kinds of health care as a public service. Taxes help to pay for health care for older people and many poor people. There are public hospitals where people can get care for free or at a low cost. Towns and cities may offer other services, such as free flu shots. And if people need emergency care, they can get help at a hospital even if they can't pay for it.

But most health care in the United States is a private service. If people don't have enough money, they may not get the help they need to stay healthy.

In a health emergency, people can get help even if they can't pay for it.

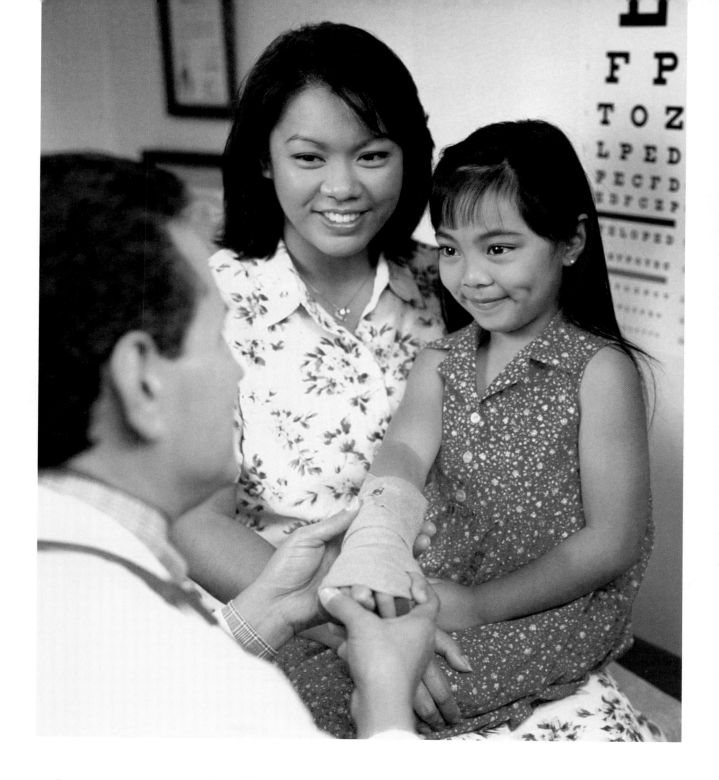

In many countries, health care is a public service for everyone. In these countries, people can see a doctor for free or for a small fee. Money from taxes helps to pay the rest of the bill. Health care is costly, so people in these countries pay higher taxes.

In many countries, health care is a public service.

These public-school students are getting a public service.

10.3 Public Schools

Do you go to a public school? If so, you are getting a public service. Money from taxes pays for public schools. The whole community pays these taxes, not just the families of students.

Public schools do a very important job for the community. Schools teach students many useful skills, such as how to read, write, and do math. Students will need these skills to get good jobs and to be helpful members of the community.

Many countries have public schools. In the United States, you can go to public schools from kindergarten through high school. After high school, you might go to a public college. You would probably have to pay part of the cost. Taxes would help pay the rest.

You can also go to a private school or college. These schools don't get money from taxes. Instead, they charge students and their families for their services.

Until about 1850, most schools in the United States were private schools. If students didn't have enough money, they didn't go to school. And in most places, only boys went to school.

Many things have changed since then. Today, people agree that everyone needs a good education. This is why communities provide schools as a public service.

Schools teach students useful skills.

10.4 Fire Fighting

Fire fighting is an important service. Putting out fires takes a lot of skill and training. It takes courage, too. Firefighters around the world often risk their lives to do their job.

Firefighters also try to keep fires from starting in the first place. They teach people what to do to prevent fires. They make sure that people obey fire safety laws.

Firefighters help communities in other ways, too. They help take care of people who are hurt in accidents. They also help people after disasters such as floods and earthquakes.

Fire fighting is an important public service.

Long ago, fire fighting wasn't a public service. When a fire broke out, everyone in town rushed to the scene. People formed a line and passed buckets of water to help put out the fire.

Two hundred and fifty years ago, some cities used volunteers to fight fires. Men formed fire-fighting clubs. The clubs had their own fire engines. The men brought buckets and other equipment.

Some places still use volunteers to fight fires. But most towns and cities hire trained fire fighters as a public service. They also buy equipment for fighting fires. Is fire fighting a public service in your community?

Long ago, people had to put out fires themselves.

10.5 Public Transportation

In towns and cities around the world, people need to get from place to place. Communities often try to help. They do this by offering public transportation.

Many cities have public buses. Some cities also have streetcars. Streetcars are small trains that use city streets. Larger cities often have subways. Subways are trains that run under the ground. Some places have trains and buses that run between cities and the **suburbs**. Suburbs are communities that grow up on the edges of cities.

Public buses are popular in London, England.

In most places, you must pay to use public transportation. But the cost is usually low so that most people can afford it.

Public transportation helps people get around without using cars. Most car engines make the air dirty. When there are fewer cars on the street, the air is cleaner.

Many cities are making it easier for people to use bicycles instead of driving cars. In some cities, you can even rent a bicycle for a low cost. Some people ride bikes to get to public buses and trains. Then they park and lock the bikes, or even bring them along for the ride.

Some people ride bikes to get to public buses.

147

10.6 Public Parks

Have you ever played in a public park? If you have, you have used a popular public service.

Why do communities spend tax money on parks? Parks bring us many benefits. They add beauty and a touch of nature to our cities and towns. Parks also give us space for all kinds of activities.

Imagine spending a sunny Saturday afternoon in a large city park. You see families having picnics and people walking their dogs. Skaters scoot along the park's paths. You see a softball game and a soccer match. You pass a band playing on an outdoor stage while people dance. In a playground area, parents talk while their children play on the swings and slides. On a pretty lake, people are rowing boats. Where else in a city can people do so many fun and healthy things?

Parks give people space for fun and healthy activities.

148

Parks are useful for another reason. They bring people together. This can help create good feelings in a community. Some parks even have community gardens. There, neighbors can work side by side growing flowers, herbs, fruits, and vegetables.

Community gardens can help bring people together.

Summary

Towns and cities offer many public services. Police and firefighters keep people safe. Health care services help people who are sick or hurt. Public schools teach students skills they need. Public transportation helps people get from place to place without using cars. Parks give people places to play and to enjoy nature. What are the public services where you live?

Benjamin Franklin, Public Servant

Today, we count on many public services. But long ago, towns and cities had few services. What famous American helped to start some needed public services? And how else did he help his city and his country?

It is 1788. A young newspaper writer sits at a table in the city of Philadelphia. The writer is a little nervous. He is about to interview one of the most famous Americans in the world: Benjamin Franklin.

Franklin is 82 years old. He has a friendly twinkle in his eyes. The writer thinks, "Maybe I shouldn't be so nervous after all!"

Let's listen as the interview begins.

Benjamin Franklin being cheered in Philadelphia

Writer: Sir, you are a hero to the readers of my newspaper. They would like to know more about your life.

Franklin: You know, I used to print my own newspapers. I am happy to talk with you.

Writer: When did you first come to Philadelphia?

Franklin: I came here in 1723. I was 17 years old. I went to work in a printer's shop. Later, I opened my own shop.

Writer: Even as a young man, you tried to solve problems in the city. What were some of them?

Franklin: One major problem was fire. Everyone used candles for light and coal for heat. Houses were made of wood. So, fires started and spread easily. I helped to start a group of volunteer firefighters. Soon other groups of firefighters started in the city. Philadelphia became a much safer place.

Young Benjamin Franklin working in a printer's shop

Franklin as a volunteer firefighter

The Granger Collection, New York

Franklin helped to start this hospital for poor people.

Writer: What were some other problems?

Franklin: Well, the streets were dirty and dark. I began a program to clean them up and add lights. Also, many sick people were poor. I raised money for a city hospital to care for them.

Writer: In 1775, the war for independence from Great Britain began. Why did you get involved?

Franklin: To protect our rights! We wanted to make our own laws and vote on our own taxes. But Britain would not let us. So I knew we had to fight. In 1776, I even helped to write the Declaration of Independence.

Writer: But what if Britain had won the war? Then people like you would have been hanged as rebels!

Franklin: That is why we Americans had to help one another. We had to hang together, or we surely would have hanged separately!

Writer: In 1776, the new American government sent you to France. Why?

Franklin: We needed France's help to win the war. I went there to ask the king for soldiers and money to buy supplies.

Writer: Wasn't it dangerous to sail to France in the middle of a war?

Franklin: Oh, yes, it was. The British could have captured our ship. Then I would have been hanged for sure! But it all turned out well. We did win the war—with France's help. And we made a new country based on the ideas of liberty and equality.

Writer: Many people say you are a wise man. What advice would you give other Americans?

Franklin: Don't think only of yourself. Think about what you can do for others. Work for the good of your community and your country. It is better to be useful than to be rich.

Franklin meeting the king of France

Who Works at City Hall?

Does your community have a **city hall**? Maybe it's called a town hall where you live. This building is where your community's government has its offices. There you'll find the people who keep your town or city running smoothly.

These people have many duties. Some of them make laws. Some make sure that the parks are clean or that the streetlights are working.

In this chapter, you'll learn about community governments. You'll visit a city called Pleasantville. You'll meet the people who work in Pleasantville's city hall, and you'll find out what they do.

11.1 The Mayor and the City Council

Most towns and cities elect people to run their governments. In Pleasantville, voters elect a mayor and a city council. The mayor is the head of the city council.

The mayor and the city council try to make Pleasantville a safe and fun place to live. Their most important job is to make laws for the city. Laws tell people what they can and cannot do. In Pleasantville, one law says people must clean up after their pets. Another law says how fast people can drive near a school.

Does your community have a city hall?

156

Many other workers help the mayor and the city council. The police help make sure that people obey the law. Firefighters help keep people safe. People in other departments have their own special work to do.

All these people need money to do their jobs. The money comes from taxes. The mayor and the city council know how much money there is to spend. They decide how much money to give to each part of the city's government.

The city council holds meetings. It makes laws for the community.

The city manager makes sure the city's work gets done.

11.2 The City Manager

The mayor and the city council make many decisions. They need someone to make sure their decisions are carried out. In Pleasantville, this is the job of the city manager.

Suppose the city council decides to have a Kids' Day. The city manager would be in charge of planning this special day. If you wanted to help with the celebration, you would talk to the city manager.

The city manager has other duties, too. One is to make a detailed plan for how to spend the city's money. This plan is called a **budget**. Another duty is to think of ways to make the city a better place to live. The city manager tells these ideas to the mayor and city council.

11.3 The City Clerk

A city clerk keeps records for a community. In Pleasantville, the city clerk keeps records of births and deaths. The city clerk also takes notes during city council meetings. Anyone can read the notes. In this way, people can always know what the council is doing.

The city clerk takes care of many other kinds of documents, too. Suppose a family wants to add a room to their house. To do this, the family needs a document called a permit. They get the permit from the city clerk.

Another important job is to help run the city's elections. The city clerk helps make sure that election laws are obeyed. The city clerk also keeps records of elections.

The city clerk keeps records for the city.

The parks and
recreation
department is
in charge of the
city's parks and
playgrounds.

11.4 The Parks and Recreation Department

Pleasantville has many parks and playgrounds. It has a public swimming pool and a city golf course. The city's parks and recreation department is in charge of these places.

Sometimes a playground needs a new slide. People might want a bike path in a city park. The showers at the public swimming pool might need to be fixed. The parks and recreation department takes care of these things.

The department also plans fun things for people to do. It organizes softball teams and swimming lessons. It even sets up community gardens around town.

11.5 The Public Library

Most towns and cities have public libraries. Libraries are good places to go when you want information or something fun to read. They have books, magazines, and newspapers. They may have music and videos, too. Often they have computers you can use.

In Pleasantville, people use public libraries in many ways. They borrow books to read at home. They use the computers to go on the Internet. They also use materials in the libraries to learn more about their local area.

The city's libraries are good for other things, too. They have story times for children. Sometimes they show movies or have concerts. They have reading groups that people can join. Sometimes writers visit to talk about their books.

Public libraries provide information and entertainment.

11.6 The Fire Department

Pleasantville has its own fire department. The fire department has two main jobs. The first job is to help people in emergencies. The city's firefighters don't just put out fires. They also help to rescue people from dangerous situations. They give medical care to people who are hurt.

The second job is to teach people what to do in an emergency. The fire department shows schools and offices how to have fire drills. Fire drills help people know what to do if a fire breaks out. The fire department also sends speakers to schools. The speakers tell students what to do in a serious situation such as an earthquake or a flood.

When a fire happens, the fire department tries to find out how it started. This helps firefighters learn more about how to prevent fires in the future.

The fire department helps to rescue people from fires and other dangers.

11.7 The Police Department

Pleasantville has a large police department. The police help to keep people safe. They do this in two main ways.

First, the police try to make sure people obey the laws. They give tickets to people who drive too fast. They try to catch people who steal or commit other crimes.

Second, the police try to stop crimes before they happen. They walk or drive through the city's neighborhoods. They want people to know they are nearby. People feel safer when they know the police are protecting them.

The police also talk to people about how to prevent crimes. They visit neighborhood groups and schools. They talk about what the police do and how people can stay safe.

The police department helps to keep people safe from crime.

11.8 The Planning Department

Cities and towns are always changing. People want to build new houses and shopping malls. They want new parks and playgrounds. Someone needs to decide which changes are best. In Pleasantville, this is the job of the planning department.

The planning department divides the city into areas called zones. Some zones are for houses. Some are for businesses. And some zones are for a mix of both.

The planning department gives permission for new buildings. It makes sure that the idea for a new building matches the city's plan. For example, the building should not cause too much traffic in a neighborhood. It should also fit in well with other buildings nearby.

The planning department makes sure that new buildings fit the city's plan.

Fixing streetlights is one of the jobs of the public works department.

11.9 The Public Works Department

Like many other cities and towns, Pleasantville has a public works department. **Public works** are things everyone uses, such as roads, water pipes, and streetlights. The department's main job is to keep public works in good shape.

People in the public works department pave roads. They fix broken streetlights and leaks in water pipes. They also build new public works. Suppose the city needs new traffic lights or sewers. First the mayor and city council vote to spend money on these projects. Then the public works department does the work.

Summary

It takes a lot of people to run a city. In Pleasantville, the mayor and the city council make the big decisions. The city manager sees that these decisions are carried out. Other people at city hall each have their own jobs to do. Together, they help to keep the city running smoothly.

One Country, Many Governments

Thousands of communities in the United States have their own governments. But we have many other governments, too. What are they? And what one law must all of them obey?

Different places have their own needs. That is why the United States has three levels of government. The **federal government** makes laws for the whole country. **State governments** make laws for each state. **Local governments** make laws for smaller areas.

In this story, you'll read about events that happened in the city of Little Rock, Arkansas. You'll see that each level of government has a job to do. But you'll also learn that there is one law that all governments in the United States must obey.

The United States has three levels of government.

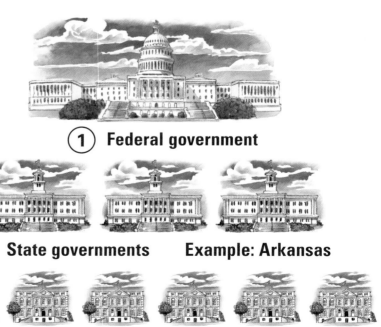

① **Federal government**

㊿ **State governments**   **Example: Arkansas**

1000's **Local governments**   **Example: Little Rock**

Trouble in Little Rock

It was September 1957. A new school year was about to start at Central High School in Little Rock, Arkansas. But it wasn't like any school year before it.

In the past, only white students could go to Central High. This year, African American students would be going there for the first time.

Many white people in the city were angry. They didn't want black students and white students going to the same schools.

The governor of Arkansas was a man named Orval Faubus. Governor Faubus was the head of the state government. He said that trouble was about to happen in Little Rock. He even warned that "blood will run in the streets" if black students tried to go to Central High. Faubus told the state **militia** to keep order in the city. A militia is made up of soldiers who serve in emergencies.

Governor Orval Faubus

Central High School

The first black students at Central High faced angry crowds.

Our Basic Law

On September 4, nine black students walked toward Central High. Hundreds of angry white people stood around the school.

Bravely, the students kept on walking. Then the state militia blocked their way. Governor Faubus had told the soldiers to keep the students out of the school.

The governor could tell the state militia what to do. But he couldn't go against the U.S. Supreme Court. The Supreme Court is part of the federal government. The Court's job is to say what the laws mean. The Court had said that keeping black and white students apart was against the U.S. Constitution.

The Constitution sets the basic rules for our government. It also protects our rights. Not even a governor can disobey it. A judge ordered Governor Faubus to let the students into the school. The governor took the soldiers away.

The President Takes Action

Once again, the black students tried to enter the school. This time, an even bigger crowd was waiting. Little Rock's city police led the students in through a side door.

The mayor of Little Rock knew that people were still very angry. He was afraid someone might get hurt. He asked U.S. president Dwight Eisenhower for help.

The president is part of the federal government. Usually, keeping the peace is the job of the local government. But the students' rights under the Constitution were in danger. This gave the president a reason to act. He sent U.S. Army troops to Little Rock to protect the black students. The students were able to go to school at last.

The story of Little Rock shows an important idea. We have many governments. Each has its own job to do. But all of them must obey the Constitution.

President Eisenhower

U.S. Army troops helped protect the students.

How Do We Have a Voice in Our Community?

Has your family ever talked about how to spend a weekend or a vacation? Did you get to say what you thought? If so, you probably felt better about the choice your family made. We all like to have a voice in the decisions that affect us.

The same is true in your town or city. People want to have a voice in the decisions that affect their lives. Also, helping to make these decisions is part of being a good **citizen**. A citizen is a person who has the right to live in a certain place. In this chapter, you'll learn about ways to make your voice heard in your community.

12.1 Going to Public Meetings

One way to have a voice in your community is to go to public meetings. Towns and cities have meetings to talk about important decisions. These decisions affect everyone who lives in the community.

Before making decisions, leaders want to know what people think. They ask people to come to public meetings to share their thoughts and ideas. For instance, leaders might call a meeting to talk about traffic safety near schools. The leaders might ask whether the city should put speed bumps on certain streets to slow cars down.

Anyone can go to a public meeting. You can go just to listen. Or you can go to share your thoughts on a topic.

People at a public meeting

If you choose to speak, the leaders of the meeting may ask you questions. When you are finished, the next person gets to speak.

It can be hard to talk in front of a group. But if you are brave enough, speaking at a public meeting will give you a voice in your community. You can tell the leaders of your town or city what you think. You can tell your neighbors, too. You might even change people's minds!

Speakers at a public meeting take turns sharing their thoughts.

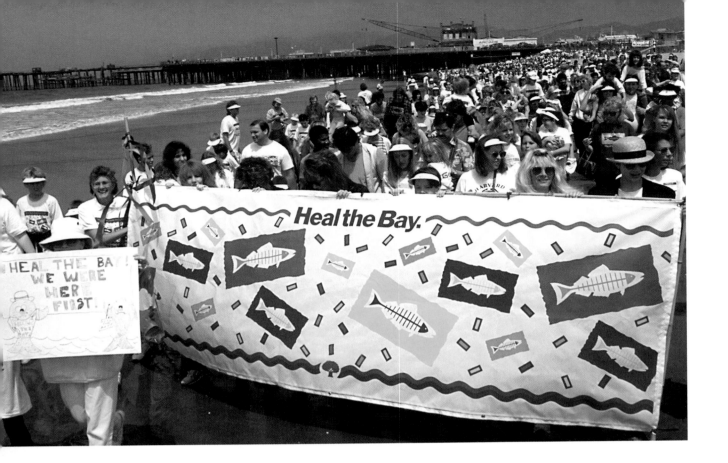

People at a peaceful
demonstration

12.2 Taking Part in Peaceful
   Demonstrations

Have you ever seen a **demonstration**? At a
demonstration, people gather to show how they feel
about an issue. A **peaceful** demonstration can be a
good way of making your voice heard. Peaceful means
not hurting others or their property.

Peaceful demonstrations let others know about a
problem. People carry signs to show how they feel.
They listen to speeches. They may chant slogans, sing
songs, or march in a parade.

In the 1950s and 1960s, there were many
demonstrations in the United States about **civil
rights**. Civil rights are rights that people have simply
because they are citizens. For instance, all adult
citizens have the right to vote.

Why were civil rights a problem in the 1950s and 1960s? At that time, many African Americans were not being given all their rights. For example, in some states, laws made it hard for them to vote.

Many people wanted this to change. Thousands of them took part in civil rights marches. These peaceful demonstrations made many Americans think more about civil rights. In time, new laws were passed to help give all citizens their rights.

A civil rights march

12.3 Supporting a Candidate

Candidates are people who run for office. This means they try to get elected to do a certain job. For example, several people may want the job of mayor. To run for this office, they become candidates.

People want to vote for candidates who will make their community a better place. So, candidates tell people about their ideas. They give speeches. They talk to news reporters. They meet voters in public places, such as shopping malls. Sometimes they even visit people's homes. Then voters choose the candidate they like best.

A candidate giving a speech

Candidates need lots of help. They can't talk to every voter. They need people to tell friends and neighbors about their ideas. They need money to send voters mail and to pay for ads on television and radio.

If you like a candidate's ideas, you can help the person get elected. This is another way to have a voice in your community.

There are many ways to support a candidate. You can give money. You can put signs in your windows or in your yard. You can talk to voters. You can help mail letters to voters. On election day, you can encourage people to vote.

Supporting a candidate is one way to make your voice heard.

12.4 Voting

Voting is one of the best ways to have a voice in your community. People vote in elections. They vote to choose community leaders. They also vote on ideas for improving their town or city.

When the United States was created, only certain people could vote. A voter had to be a white man who owned land. Over time, more and more people won the right to vote.

There are still a few rules about who can vote. Voters must be at least 18 years old. They must be citizens of the United States. And they must **register**, or sign up, to vote.

People vote by marking a **ballot**. The ballot lists all the candidates and ideas to vote on. After everyone has voted, the ballots are counted to see which candidates and ideas have won.

People must register before they can vote.

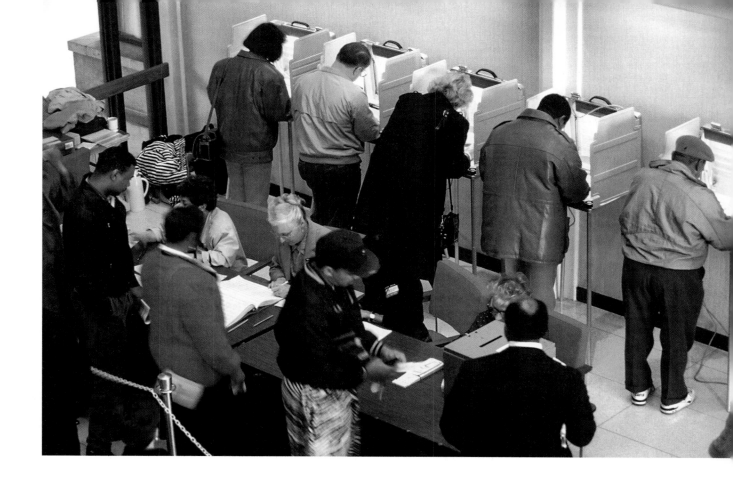

People voting on election day

Today, some people vote by mail. But most people vote in person on election day. They mark their ballots in small booths. The booths keep other people from seeing how they are voting.

Leaders make most of the decisions for a community. But in an election, every voter helps to choose ideas and candidates. In this way, voting gives people a strong voice in their community.

Summary

You can make your voice heard in your community in many ways. You can go to public meetings. You can take part in peaceful demonstrations. You can help candidates. And when you turn 18, you can vote.

Making Your Voice Count

Voting gives you a voice in your community—and your country. But voting is more than just marking a ballot. What steps are involved in being a good voter?

It was a big day at Alf's school. The school was taking part in a national mock election for president of the United States. A mock election is a pretend election held for practice. The election was big news in town.

Outside his classroom, Alf saw Anna Wong. She was a reporter from the local television station.

"Are you voting in the mock election?" Ms. Wong asked.

"I sure am!" Alf answered.

"Voting is a big responsibility," Ms. Wong said. "Can you tell me how you got ready for the election?"

"Sure," Alf answered.

These students are about to vote in a mock election.

"The first step was to register to vote," Alf explained. "The deadline was two weeks before the election. Some students put up signs in the halls reminding everyone to register. If we signed up by the deadline, we got a special sticker."

"What was the next step?" Ms. Wong asked.

"The second step was research," Alf said. "We had to find out what the candidates were like and what they would do if they got elected. So we read about them on the Internet. We read articles in newspapers.

"We also had Meet the Candidates events. Those were cool. One student would play the part of a candidate. Another student would play the part of a reporter and ask questions. The rest of us tried to decide which candidate had the best ideas."

Registering to vote

Doing research

Marking sample ballots

"It sounds like you really prepared well," Ms. Wong said. "So then were you ready to vote?"

"Not yet," Alf answered. "The third step was to learn how to mark the ballot. Our teacher gave us sample ballots. She said voters in real elections get them, too. We used them to learn how to mark our choices correctly. I marked my sample ballot today. That way, I'll know just what to do when I get in the voting booth."

Ms. Wong looked surprised. "You even have voting booths?" she asked.

"Sure," said Alf. "We made them out of cardboard and set them up in our classroom. Hey, I'd better get going! It's time for the last step."

"What's that?" asked Ms. Wong.

Alf grinned. "Voting for president!" he called as he disappeared into his classroom.

Ms. Wong thought about what she would say on the evening news. She would tell people that that the students were very excited about voting for president. Of course, their votes wouldn't count in the real election. But everyone in town would know how the vote came out. In this way, the students would be making their voices heard.

"I'll say something else, too," Ms. Wong thought. "I'll tell people how hard the students worked to get ready for the election. They understand that voting isn't just a right. It's a responsibility. It's something we should do with care."

Just then, Alf came out of the classroom. He was wearing a big sticker that said, "I Voted Today."

"I can't wait until I'm 18," Alf told her. "Voting today was fun. But one day my vote can help change the country!"

Voting

BALLOT BOX

Whose Planet Is It, Anyway?

We all want our planet to be a safe and healthy place. That's why we need to take care of the **environment**. The environment includes Earth's air, water, soil, and living things.

How do we protect the environment? One way is to solve problems such as **pollution**. Pollution is anything that makes air, water, or soil dirty or unsafe.

Pollution has many causes. Cars and factories send smoke into the air. Ships may spill oil into the ocean. Sometimes dangerous chemicals are dumped into the ground. In this chapter, you will read about how three communities tried to solve these problems.

13.1 Air Pollution

Tara Church was eight years old when she started to worry about air pollution. It all started with paper plates. Tara was a Brownie in the Girl Scouts. She and her Brownie friends were planning to take paper plates on a camping trip.

"We won't have to wash the plates," the girls said. "That way, we'll save water."

"Here's another thing to think about," said Tara's mother. "Paper is made from trees. Using paper plates means more trees have to be cut down."

"Why is that important?" asked one of the girls.

"Trees help to take smoke and chemicals out of the air," Tara's mother said. "They help fight air pollution."

Trees help to fight air pollution.

Tara and her friends knew about air pollution. They lived in El Segundo, a town near Los Angeles in southern California. Some days, the sky turned a dirty brown. Sometimes the air had a bad smell.

El Segundo is near busy freeways. Car engines are a big cause of air pollution. Los Angeles International Airport is also close by. Airplanes burn lots of fuel when they take off. They cause air pollution, too. Factories nearby send smoke into the air. That can make the problem even worse.

"It isn't good to breathe air pollution," Tara and her friends agreed. "But what can a bunch of third graders do about it?"

Sometimes the air near Los Angeles turned a dirty brown.

187

Planting trees is a good way to help keep the air clean.

13.2 Tree Musketeers to the Rescue

After thinking about the problem, the girls had an idea. "We should plant a tree!" they said.

The girls planted a tree they called "Marcie the Marvelous Tree." But they didn't stop there. "One tree won't clean up that much pollution," they told each other. "Let's get other kids to plant lots of trees, too."

The girls decided to form a group called the Tree Musketeers. The group began planting trees in El Segundo in 1987. Before long, the group had planted more than 700 trees.

Like a healthy young tree, the girls' idea kept growing. As time went on, new kids got involved in the Tree Musketeers. By 2008, more than one million kids had planted more than a million trees!

Today's Tree Musketeers have another reason to help clean the air. Some kinds of air pollution help to trap heat from the sun. Scientists say that this adds to **global warming**. Global warming is a rise in Earth's temperature over time. Many scientists worry that too much warming would harm the environment in many ways. They say that some crops and other plants might not grow as well. Some animals might die out. Some places could have more hot spells, less water, and stronger storms.

Scientists disagree about how harmful global warming might be. But one thing is sure—trees can help! Trees soak up a gas called carbon dioxide. This gas is one of the main kinds of pollution that trap the sun's heat. That's why the Tree Musketeers say they are fighting global warming by planting trees.

MARCIE
THE MARVELOUS TREE

BORN MAY 9, 1987

OUT OF CONCERN
BY THE CHILDREN
FOR THE ENVIRONMENT
AND THEIR HOPE FOR THE FUTURE

THE TREE MUSKETEERS

Marcie has become a famous tree. This sign tells visitors why Marcie was planted.

13.3 A Huge Oil Spill

It was just after midnight on March 24, 1989. A huge oil tanker moved through the waters off the coast of Alaska. A tanker is a ship that carries liquid or gas.

The oil tanker was called the *Exxon Valdez*. It was almost as long as three football fields. It carried more than 53 million gallons of oil.

Suddenly, disaster struck. The man steering the ship became tired or careless. He failed to keep the tanker in safe shipping lanes. The ship ran into a reef that lay under the water. The reef punched a hole in the ship. Oil began leaking into the water.

The *Exxon Valdez*

In all, about 11 million gallons of oil spread through the water. Birds and other animals got covered in oil. The oil ruined their feathers and fur. They couldn't stay warm. Some of them began to freeze to death.

As the creatures tried to clean themselves, they swallowed some of the oil. The oil poisoned many of them.

People in Alaska were worried and angry. Thick, sticky oil coated about 1,300 miles of the Alaska shore. Thousands of birds and other animals were sick and dying.

"What can we do about this?" people asked. "And how can we make sure it never happens again?"

The oil spread through the water and coated beaches.

13.4 Stopping Oil Spills

After the oil spill, people did their best to clean up the mess. Rescuers rushed to save birds and other animals. Thousands of workers began trying to clean up the water and beaches.

But nothing could solve all the problems caused by the oil spill. The spill killed more than 250,000 seabirds. About 3,000 otters died. So did 300 seals and about 13 killer whales. Some of the oil can still be found in the water and on beaches today.

The best solution to oil spills is to keep them from happening in the first place. So the U.S. government took action. It passed a law saying that oil tankers in Alaska must have stronger walls.

Workers tried to clean the beaches and save birds and animals.

Other laws were passed to make sure companies and their workers act more safely. The government also punished the company that owned the tanker. The company agreed to pay millions of dollars in fines. Some of the money helped to pay for the cleanup.

The ship's captain was punished, too. He had to pay a fine of $50,000. He also had to spend many hours helping the communities.

Communities in Alaska are doing their part. Today they are ready to help clean up if another big oil spill happens. But everyone hopes it never does.

Today, workers practice ways to clean up the water after an oil spill.

193

13.5 Schools and Toxic Waste

Kim grew up in Marion, Ohio. When she was 28, she became very sick with a rare kind of cancer.

A few years later, other people in town started getting cancer. All of them had gone to Kim's school, River Valley High School.

Some people began to wonder why so many people in Marion had cancer. They wondered if something at the high school was causing people who had been students there to get sick.

Kim's parents joined a group called Concerned River Valley Families. The group demanded that scientists test the school grounds.

It turned out that the soil under the high school contained **toxic waste**. The word *toxic* means "poisonous." *Waste* means "trash" or "garbage."

The toxic waste in Marion came from the U.S. Army. Years before, the army had used the land as a place to dump chemicals. The school was built right on top of this toxic waste dump.

River Valley
High School

Toxic waste can make land unhealthy even when the waste is covered up.

At first the army said the land was safe. So did the government of Ohio. The scientists said they didn't know what caused the kind of cancer Kim had, so the toxic waste couldn't be blamed.

The parents in the Concerned Families group disagreed. They said, "We can't take chances with our children's health. The school is not safe!"

13.6 Making Sure Schools Are Safe

The Concerned River Valley Families wanted to close the high school. They talked to the people in charge of the school. They went to public meetings. They made sure that news reporters wrote about the problem.

Thanks to these families, the story made news around the country. Lois Gibbs even came to visit. Do you remember her? She was the mother who spoke up about the dangerous chemicals at Love Canal.

In the end, the families won their fight. The high school was closed, and a new school was built in another location.

Did toxic waste cause Kim and other people from her school to get cancer? No one knows for sure. But many scientists say that toxic waste is especially dangerous to growing children. For this reason, many people want to make sure that schools are safe from toxic chemicals.

Roxanne Krumanaker was one of the parents who fought to close River Valley High School.

Around the country, parents are taking action. They have stopped some schools from being built on old garbage dumps. They have worked to close schools where dangerous chemicals have been found. And they have demanded new laws to protect children from toxic waste.

These parents are a lot like the Tree Musketeers. They think that pollution is everyone's problem. And they think that everyone can be part of the solution.

Summary

Many people have tried to solve pollution problems. The Tree Musketeers planted trees to fight air pollution. The government and local communities have worked to lessen the harm caused by oil spills. Parents made sure people knew about toxic waste near schools. What might you do to help solve a pollution problem where you live?

Finding New Sources of Energy

Fighting pollution is one way to help the environment. Another way is to find new sources of energy. Where do we get the energy that lights our homes and fuels our cars? And how can new sources of energy help our planet?

The teams were ready. The students placed their model cars behind the starting line. Each car was less than two feet long.

A loud voice rang out. "On your mark, get set, go!" The race began.

The small cars sped down the racetrack. The students held their breath. Which teams would win awards for building the fastest cars? Which would win for the best designs?

What is special about the cars in this race?

This house uses solar panels to collect energy from sunlight.

All car races are exciting, but this one was special. It was part of the National Junior Solar Sprint. Teams of middle school students take part in this event. Each team builds a model car that runs only on solar energy. This type of energy comes from sunlight. Then the teams race their cars down a track.

Why would students build cars that use energy from the sun? One reason is to have fun. Another reason is to learn about **renewable resources**.

Renewable means that we can get more of something. Some energy comes from renewable resources like sunlight, wind, or water. This kind of resource isn't used up. We can get more of it in a short time because we always have sunlight, wind, and water.

Coal must be dug out of the ground.

Why is getting energy from renewable resources important? We use lots of energy every day. Energy keeps our houses warm in winter and cool in summer. Energy lights our rooms and runs our computers and televisions. It fuels our cars, buses, and airplanes.

We get most of this energy from sources that lie under the ground. These include coal, oil, and natural gas. These resources are called **fossil fuels**. Fossil fuels come from the fossils, or remains, of plants and animals. These remains have been buried in Earth for millions of years.

Someday we will use up these resources. So, they are called **nonrenewable resources**. These resources cannot be made again in a short time. Because of this, we need more energy sources.

Burning fossil fuels adds pollution to the air.

There is a second reason to find new energy sources. Coal, oil, and gas must be burned to make power. Burning fossil fuels can make the air unhealthy to breathe. Burning these fuels also puts more carbon dioxide in the air. This can add to global warming.

Using energy from sunlight, wind, and water doesn't pollute the air. But getting this energy is challenging. We don't yet know how to get all the energy we need from renewable sources. And right now it's very expensive to turn these forms of energy into power we can use.

Will these Junior Solar Sprint champions help find new sources of energy?

That's why the Junior Solar Sprint is so exciting. Racing model cars is just a first step. Some of these students may become scientists and engineers. One day, they could help to find new ways to bring us the energy we need.

How Can We Help the Global Community?

We are all part of many communities. Some communities are small, like your school. Others are much bigger, like your state. The largest community of all is the **global community**. Everyone on Earth is a member of this community. So are animals and other living things. We all share our planet's water, air, and soil. We all depend on each other to have healthy and happy lives.

It's up to us to take care of the global community. This chapter has lots of ideas for ways to share our Earth. How many others can you think of?

14.1 Help Fight Air Pollution

In Chapter 13, you learned how some people have tried to protect the environment. Let's look at some ways you can help.

One way to protect the environment is to fight air pollution. Cars are a major source of air pollution. So, you can help reduce air pollution by cutting down on how much you ride in cars.

Often, there are other ways of getting where you want to go. Instead of riding in a car, you might be able to take a bus, a train, or a subway. Maybe you could ride a bike. Or you could walk.

Do you still need a car to get where you are going? Try to find other people who are going to the same place. Then you can ride together in one car.

Using cars less helps to fight air pollution.

14.2 Make Less Waste

A second way to help protect the environment is to make less waste. Most of our garbage goes into dumps called landfills. Many people worry that the waste in landfills can harm our air, soil, and water. And some places are running out of room to build new landfills.

How can you make less waste? Keep in mind the three R's: reduce, reuse, and recycle.

Reduce means to use less of things that will make waste. For example, your family can make less cardboard waste by buying one large box of cereal instead of several small ones. Your family can reduce toxic waste, too. When you buy products such as household cleaners, look for ones that don't have toxic chemicals in them.

Reuse means to use things more than once. Use both sides of a sheet of paper before you recycle it. Try making arts and crafts from materials instead of throwing them away.

Is there a recycling program where you live?

Recycle means to save waste so it can be used again to make new products. In most places, you can recycle cans, bottles, newspapers, and other materials.

205

14.3 Help Save Energy and Water

A third way to help protect the environment is to save precious resources. Two of these resources are energy and water.

Remember, nonrenewable sources of energy cannot be replaced in a short time. And even fresh water may become scarce in the future.

You can help. Use energy wisely. Turn off lights when you leave a room. Turn off televisions and computers when no one is using them. In cold weather, put on a sweater and turn down the heat.

Use water wisely, too. Take shorter showers. Don't leave the water running when you brush your teeth. If you have a hose, use a nozzle you can turn off when you lay the hose down. Tell your school or city about sprinklers that are broken or that are watering the sidewalk instead of grass and plants.

14.4 Help Keep Animals Safe

We share the planet with many kinds of wildlife. Birds and other animals need our help to survive.

Here are three ways you can help keep animals safe—even animals that live far away from you.

First, buy dolphin-safe tuna. Some nets used to catch tuna also trap and kill dolphins. But most nets are designed to allow dolphins to escape. Your family can help save dolphins by buying tuna that says "dolphin safe" on the label.

Second, don't buy products made from endangered animals. Some examples are coats made from fur, decorations made with ivory from elephants, and belts made of alligator skins.

Third, find out about dangers to wildlife in your area. For example, some chemicals used on grass and other plants can poison birds. If you have a garden or yard, learn how to make it a safer place for wildlife.

14.5 Help Save Animal Habitats

You can also help animals by saving their **habitats**. Habitats are places where particular animals live, such as the forest or the seashore.

We often spoil animal habitats with our trash. Drinks are sometimes sold with plastic rings that hold bottles or cans together. Birds and other animals can get tangled in these rings. Animals can also choke on old balloons and other litter. Plastic bags that get washed into the ocean can harm fish and birds. So, don't be a litterbug! Even better, take along a trash bag when you go to a park or a beach. Pick up any litter you find.

You can also support groups that work to save animal habitats around the world. You can find many of these groups on the Internet. Some groups even have kids' clubs you can join.

Picking up litter is one way to help wildlife.

14.6 Share with Other People

People in friendly communities help one another. Nearly all of us can do something to help others in our global community.

One way to help is by sharing the things we have. If you have old clothes, don't throw them away. Maybe someone else in your family can use the clothes you've outgrown. Or you can give them to groups that collect clothes for people in need.

Other groups collect food or toys for families who can't afford to buy them. You may have seen collection barrels at your supermarket or school. Don't pass them by! You might have canned food in your kitchen that your family can give away. Or you might be able to save up to buy a toy or some food. Even one can of food can be a big help to someone.

Do you have food drives where you live?

14.7 Lend a Helping Hand

Many groups bring people together to lend others a helping hand. You can help others by joining a group that's right for you.

One such group might be UNICEF (pronounced YOO-nih-sehf). UNICEF helps needy children around the world. Every Halloween, thousands of kids in the United States trick-or-treat to collect money for UNICEF instead of candy for themselves.

One town in California has a group called Kids Cheering Kids. Kids in this group give some of their free time to help other kids. They visit sick children in hospitals. They help students with schoolwork. They spend time with children in homeless shelters. If you can't find a group like this to join, maybe you can start one!

UNICEF sends help to children around the world.

14.8 Treat Others with Respect

Everyone needs respect. You can make a big difference just by being **tolerant** of others. Being tolerant means respecting people even if they're different from you.

It's hurtful to make fun of others or to harm them because of how they look, dress, or talk. Act kindly instead. If you see people who are not being tolerant of others, speak up. Remind them that everyone deserves respect.

Take time to learn about other people. The more you know about others, the more you will respect them. Talk to new people in your school or town. You might even try becoming pen pals with a child in another country.

Summary

We are all members of the global community. It is up to us to help make our world a better place. We can help the environment. We can help wildlife. We can help other people. What will you do?

Learning About Others Through Art

Many countries share our Earth. These countries need to get along to make a true global community. But people sometimes dislike or fear those who live in other places. How can art help people around the world learn about one another?

A painting of women in China

People in different countries have different ways of life. They have their own governments and laws. They speak their own languages. It can be hard for them to know what people in other places are like.

Think of China and the United States. As you know, China is in Asia. Thousands of miles of ocean lie between China and the United States. Most Chinese will never see the United States. Most Americans will never see China. So how can people in these places get to know one another? One way is through art.

Look at the painting on the facing page. It shows a group of women in China. They are dressed in traditional Chinese clothing. What does this scene tell you about Chinese culture? How is the scene like one that you might see in the United States? How is it different?

A painting of a girl in China

The painting was made by a Chinese artist named Hu Jundi. People all over the world collect his paintings. Why do you think Hu Jundi's work is so popular in other countries?

The painting of a girl on this page also comes from China. What can you guess about the girl from details in the painting? What can you guess about the artist? What might he want you to feel about this girl?

Both of these paintings are now in the United States. When Americans see these pictures, they learn about people in China and about their lives. What are some things Americans might learn that they didn't know before?

A painting of Daniel Boone leading settlers through the mountains

People in China are also learning about life in the United States. In 2007, an art student named Song Wei went to an art show in China. More than 100 paintings were on display. They showed scenes in the United States from the year 1700 to today.

One painting showed George Washington. Another showed Daniel Boone. He was a famous pioneer. In the painting, Boone is leading settlers through a gap in some mountains.

Visitors like Song Wei also saw a painting of the Statue of Liberty. They saw a painting of a clown with a drum. One picture showed a big sign saying "Hollywood." Hollywood is famous for being a place where American movies are made.

Song Wei was excited. People in China had never seen so much American art in one show. Song Wei said the show "gives us a good chance to learn."

Learning is what shows like these are all about. That is why the governments of China and the United States have agreed to share their art with each other. Art can teach us about other cultures. It can show us what is different and special about another country. Art can also show us how much we have in common with other people around the world.

In this way, art can help the world's people understand one another better. This may help us live together more peacefully as part of the global community.

American art being shown in China

At School

Citizenship Throughout the Day

In the Community

At Home

What Citizenship Means

In Chapter 12, you learned that a citizen is someone who has a right to live in a certain place. If you were born in the United States, then you are a U.S. citizen. If your parents are U.S. citizens, then you are, too. Does your family come from another country? If so, you may be a citizen of that country, this country, or both!

Citizens have many other rights as well. In fact, the United States was started by people who wanted to protect their rights. The Constitution lists many of these rights. But being a citizen doesn't just mean having rights. Citizens have responsibilities, too. For example, citizens must obey the law. Most must pay taxes. And all citizens must respect the values of our country. You promise to do this whenever you say the Pledge of Allegiance or sing the national anthem.

The Pledge of Allegiance is a promise to respect the values that the flag stands for.

A big part of citizenship is doing our share to protect the things that all of us need and care about. We call these things the **common good**. For instance, we all want our communities to be clean. If just one person litters, it spoils things for everyone. If people didn't pay taxes, then we wouldn't have money to pay for public services.

Look at the chart on this page. It shows some of the main rights and responsibilities of U.S. citizens. Together, these rights and responsibilities make up the idea of **citizenship**. A few, such as the right to vote, will apply to you when you are old enough. But most of them are part of your life right now. Let's take a closer look at how you can show good citizenship every day.

Some Rights and Responsibilities of U.S. Citizens	
Rights	**Responsibilities**
• To speak freely • To practice the religion of your choice • To gather peacefully with other people • To own property • To be safe from harm • To vote • To have a trial by jury	• To be loyal to your country and its values, especially freedom and equality • To care for the common good • To obey the law • To respect the rights and property of others • To pay taxes • To vote • To serve on juries

At School

During the school year, you spend a big part of your day at school. You have many chances to show good citizenship during this time.

To begin with, you can obey the rules. Schools have rules for the same reason that communities have laws. Rules help people get along. They protect both the common good and each person's rights. For instance, your school probably has rules about treating other people and their property with respect. And you have the right to be treated with respect, too.

Taking part in making decisions is a big part of citizenship. Do you elect leaders for your class, or for clubs or groups? Do you sometimes get to vote on projects or rules for your class or your school? Do you listen carefully to other people's points of view? If so, you're practicing good citizenship.

Voting is a big part of citizenship.

Helping younger students is one way to be a good citizen at school.

You can also do things for the common good. Could some of your schoolmates use a helping hand? Are there problems at your school that you can help solve? Here are a few examples of things that students like you have done:

- Students at one school created illustrated books for kindergarteners. The books helped the young children learn about their new school.

- A group of third graders had a problem with bullies on the school bus. The third graders designed a program for bus safety. They worked together with older students, school officials, parents, and bus drivers.

- Many students tutor younger students in reading and other subjects.

Your school may have other projects or programs you can get involved in. Or you could start one yourself. Being a leader is another way to show good citizenship.

In the Community

You spend part of almost every day out in your community. Even if you're just going shopping or to a playground, you have both rights and responsibilities. For example, you have the right to speak and act freely as long as you respect the rights of others. You have a responsibility to obey the law. You have a responsibility to respect others' property.

Some of your rights and responsibilities will change as you get older. When you have a job, you'll pay taxes on money you earn. As an adult, you will sometimes be expected to serve on a jury. A jury is a group of citizens who decide a case in court. You'll also have the right—and the responsibility—to vote. You may work to help elect a candidate. You may even run for office yourself.

Members of a jury listen to a lawyer in court.

Meanwhile, you can start right now to work for the common good in your town or city. You might work on a project such as helping to clean up a public park. Or you might start your own project. One group of third graders made a map of the safety features in their neighborhood. The map showed things like fire hydrants and telephones. Another group of students worked at a soup kitchen. They spent a day giving out food to hungry and homeless people.

You can also show citizenship by taking part in patriotic activities. **Patriotism** means love of your country. Many patriotic activities take place on holidays. Learn the meaning of each holiday. Then think about how to show your patriotism on these days. Even going to see a Fourth of July parade in your community can be an act of citizenship.

Sometimes being a good citizen can be fun!

Some Major Holidays in the United States

Holiday	Date	Purpose of Holiday
Martin Luther King Jr. Day	3rd Monday in January	To honor the birthday of civil rights leader Martin Luther King Jr.
Presidents' Day	3rd Monday in February	To honor all past U.S. presidents
Memorial Day	Last Monday in May	To remember Americans killed in wars
Independence Day	July 4	To celebrate the approval of the Declaration of Independence
Labor Day	1st Monday in September	To honor the country's working people
Columbus Day	2nd Monday in October	To remember the day Christopher Columbus arrived in North America
Veterans Day	November 11	To honor Americans who have fought in wars
Thanksgiving Day	4th Thursday in November	To remember a feast of thanksgiving held by the Pilgrims (early settlers) and American Indians in 1621

At Home

You begin and end most days at home. Would you be surprised to find out that citizenship is part of your day there, too?

You probably have some rules at home. These rules help people live together, just as rules and laws do at school and in your community. So your first responsibility is to obey the rules.

A second responsibility is to show respect for others' rights and property. Help to take care of the space you share with others. It's the same idea as helping to keep the community clean so everyone can enjoy it.

Good citizens need to be able to cooperate. They must learn to listen to other points of view. They must learn to compromise for the common good. And they must learn to settle disagreements peacefully. You can practice all these parts of citizenship at home.

At home, good citizenship can mean helping out with chores.

For this family, dinnertime is a chance to talk about the news of the day.

You can also help your family do its part in the community. For example, good citizens know what is happening in their community. They read or watch the news. They talk about the problems of the day. You may be able to help encourage this part of citizenship in your home.

That is just what one group of students did. They created a plan to encourage discussions during their families' dinnertimes. First, they brainstormed questions for the family to talk about during dinner. Then, they brought the questions home. Community organizations loved the idea, so they helped to support it.

As you can see, you can make citizenship a part of your life throughout the day. By now you probably have some ideas of your own. Why don't you write them down and start acting on them—today?

The Pledge of Allegiance

I pledge allegiance to the flag of the United States of America and to the republic for which it stands, one nation under God, indivisible, with liberty and justice for all.

The Star-Spangled Banner

Francis Scott Key wrote the words to "The Star-Spangled Banner" in 1814. The U.S. Congress made this song our national anthem in 1931. Here is the first verse.

O! say can you see by the dawn's early light,
What so proudly we hailed at the twilight's last gleaming,
Whose broad stripes and bright stars through the perilous fight,
O'er the ramparts we watch'd, were so gallantly streaming?
And the rockets' red glare, the bombs bursting in air,
Gave proof through the night that our flag was still there;
O! say does that star-spangled banner yet wave,
O'er the land of the free, and the home of the brave?

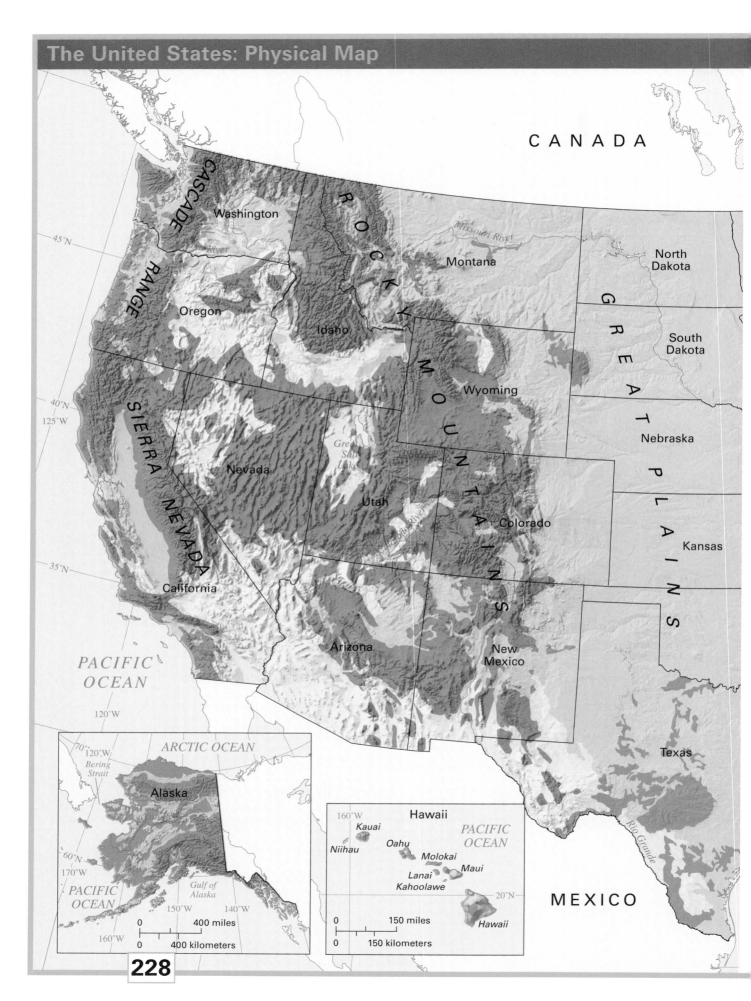

CANADA

CASCADE RANGE

Washington

Columbia River

45°N

Missouri River

Montana

North Dakota

R O C K Y

Oregon

Idaho

G R E A T

South Dakota

SIERRA NEVADA

40°N
125°W

M O U N T A I N S

Wyoming

Great Salt Lake

Nevada

Nebraska

Utah

Colorado

P L A I N S

Kansas

California

35°N

Colorado River

Arizona

New Mexico

PACIFIC OCEAN

120°W

Texas

Rio Grande

ARCTIC OCEAN

70°N
120°W

Bering Strait

Alaska

Hawaii

160°W

Kauai

PACIFIC OCEAN

60°N

Niihau

Oahu

Molokai

170°W

Lanai

Maui

PACIFIC OCEAN

150°W   140°W

Gulf of Alaska

Kahoolawe

20°N

MEXICO

160°W

0   400 miles

0   400 kilometers

0   150 miles

0   150 kilometers

Hawaii

228

0   250   500 miles

0   250   500 kilometers

N
NW   NE
W   E
SW   SE
S

Gulf of St. Lawrence

St. Lawrence River

Maine

Vermont

New Hampshire

Lake Superior

Minnesota

Wisconsin

Michigan

Lake Michigan

Lake Huron

Lake Ontario

New York

Massachusetts

Lake Erie

Rhode Island
Connecticut

Mississippi River

Iowa

Illinois

Indiana

Ohio

Pennsylvania

New Jersey

Delaware

Maryland

Missouri River

Missouri

Ohio River

Kentucky

West Virginia

Virginia

70°W

APPALACHIAN MOUNTAINS

North Carolina

Oklahoma

Arkansas

Tennessee

Mississippi River

South Carolina

ATLANTIC OCEAN

Mississippi

Alabama

Georgia

Louisiana

Florida

75°W

Gulf of Mexico

95°W   90°W   85°W   80°W

Mountain

Forest

Desert

Plain

The United States: Political Map

CANADA

Washington
★ Olympia

45°N

★ Salem

Oregon

Helena ★
Montana

North
Dakota

Bismarck ★

★ Boise
Idaho

South
Dakota

Pierre ★

40°N
125°W

Wyoming

Cheyenne ★

Nebraska

Sacramento ★

★ Carson City

Nevada

Salt Lake
City ★

Utah

★ Denver

Colorado

California

Kansas

35°N

Santa Fe ★

Oklahoma
City ★

Arizona

★ Phoenix

New Mexico

PACIFIC
OCEAN

120°W

Texas

Austin ★

ARCTIC OCEAN
70°N

Alaska

160°W

Hawaii

Kauai

PACIFIC
OCEAN

Niihau

Oahu

60°N
170°W

Honolulu ★

Molokai

Maui

PACIFIC
OCEAN

150°W 140°W

Juneau ★

Lanai
Kahoolawe

20°N

MEXICO

160°W

Hawaii

0   400 miles

0   400 kilometers

0   150 miles

0   150 kilometers

230

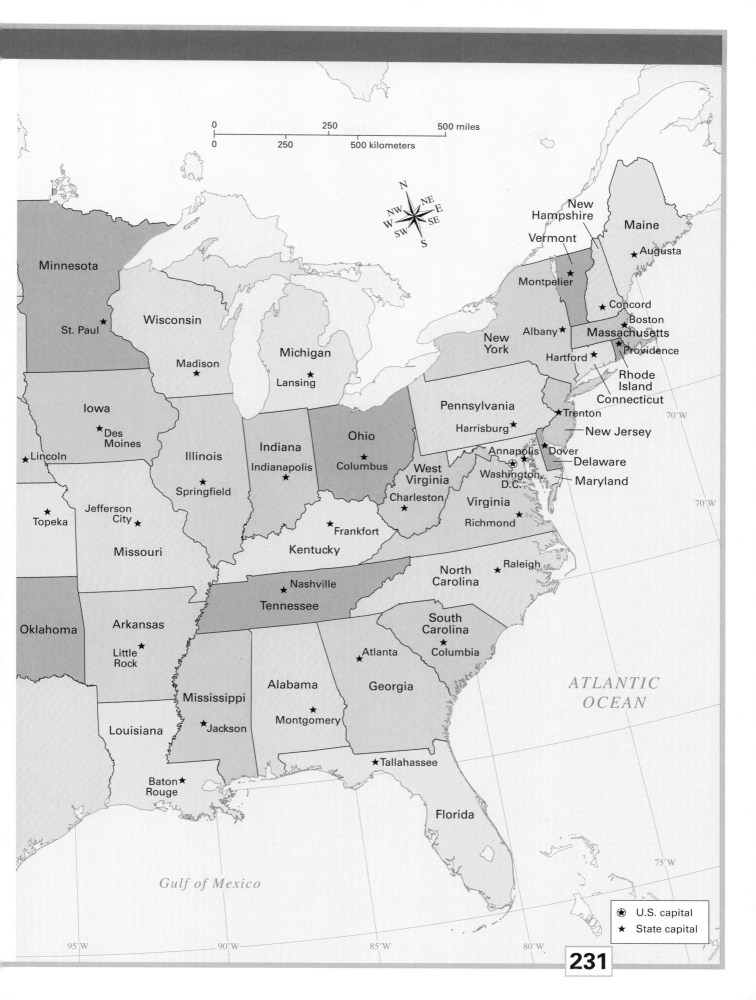

0   250   500 miles

0   250   500 kilometers

N
NE
NW   E
W   SE
SW
S

Maine

★ Augusta

New Hampshire

Vermont

★ Montpelier

★ Concord

★ Boston

Massachusetts

Minnesota

★ St. Paul

Wisconsin

★ Madison

Michigan

★ Lansing

New York

Albany ★

Hartford ★

★ Providence

Rhode Island

Connecticut

Iowa

★ Des Moines

★ Lincoln

Illinois

★ Springfield

Indiana

Indianapolis ★

Ohio

★ Columbus

Pennsylvania

Harrisburg ★

★ Trenton

New Jersey

Annapolis ★

★ Dover

Delaware

⊛ Washington, D.C.

Maryland

West Virginia

Charleston ★

Virginia

Richmond ★

★ Topeka

Jefferson City ★

Missouri

★ Frankfort

Kentucky

Oklahoma

Arkansas

Little Rock ★

Nashville ★

Tennessee

North Carolina

★ Raleigh

South Carolina

★ Columbia

Mississippi

★ Jackson

Alabama

★ Montgomery

Atlanta ★

Georgia

Louisiana

Baton Rouge ★

★ Tallahassee

Florida

ATLANTIC OCEAN

Gulf of Mexico

70°W

70°W

75°W

95°W   90°W   85°W   80°W

⊛ U.S. capital

★ State capital

231

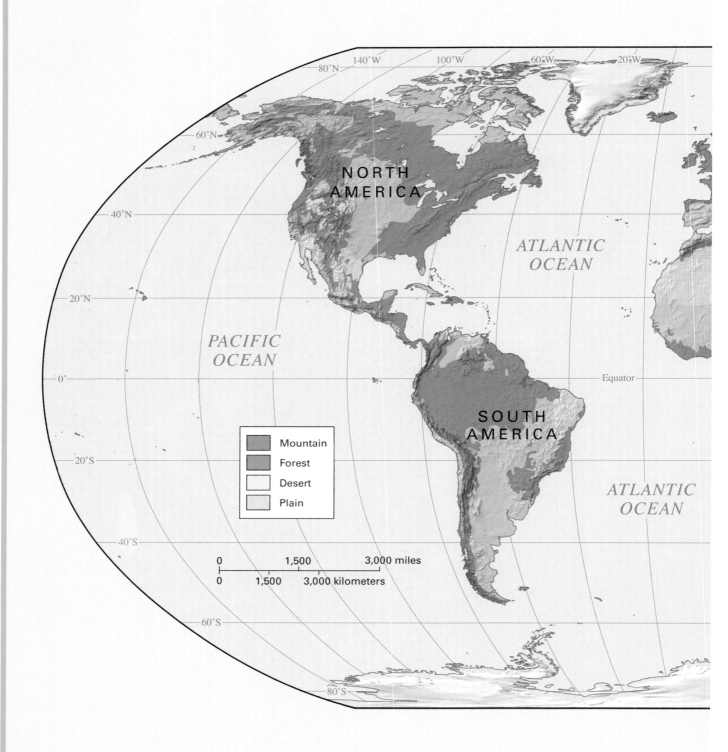

NORTH
AMERICA

ATLANTIC
OCEAN

PACIFIC
OCEAN

SOUTH
AMERICA

ATLANTIC
OCEAN

Equator

80°N
140°W   100°W   60°W   20°W
60°N
40°N
20°N
0°
20°S
40°S
60°S
80°S

Mountain
Forest
Desert
Plain

0   1,500   3,000 miles
0   1,500   3,000 kilometers

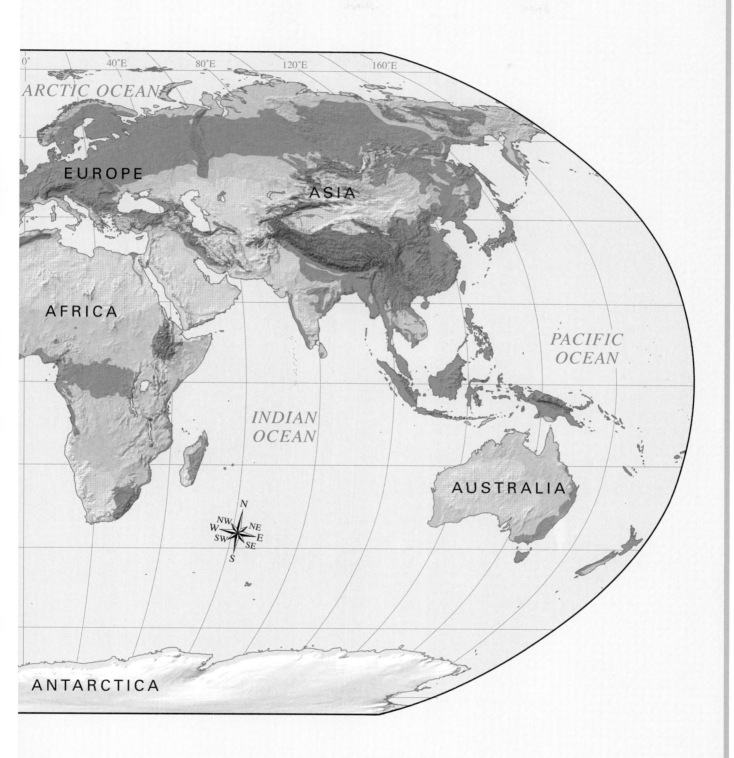

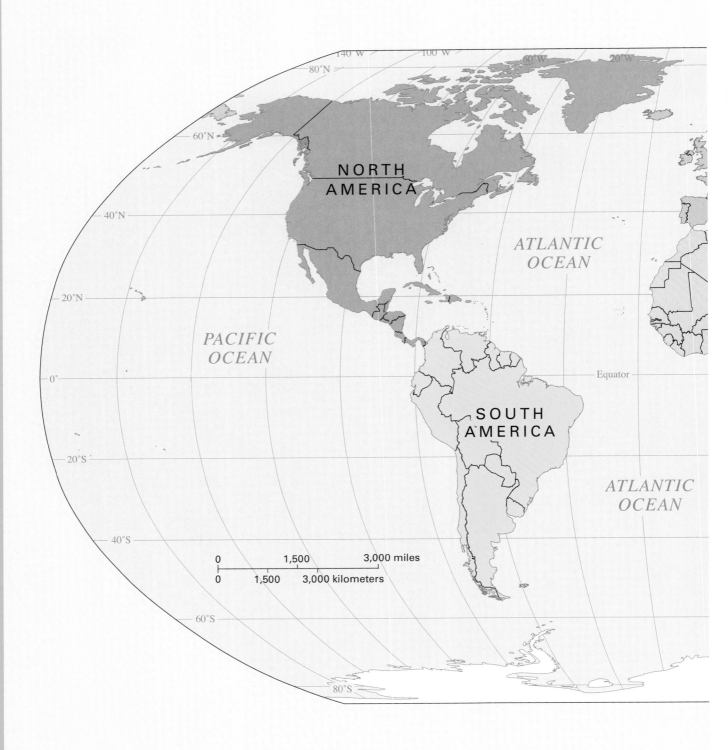

140 W 100 W 60 W 20 W

80°N

60°N

NORTH
AMERICA

40°N

ATLANTIC
OCEAN

20°N

PACIFIC
OCEAN

0°

Equator

SOUTH
AMERICA

20°S

ATLANTIC
OCEAN

40°S

| 0 | 1,500 | 3,000 miles |
| 0 | 1,500 | 3,000 kilometers |

60°S

80°S

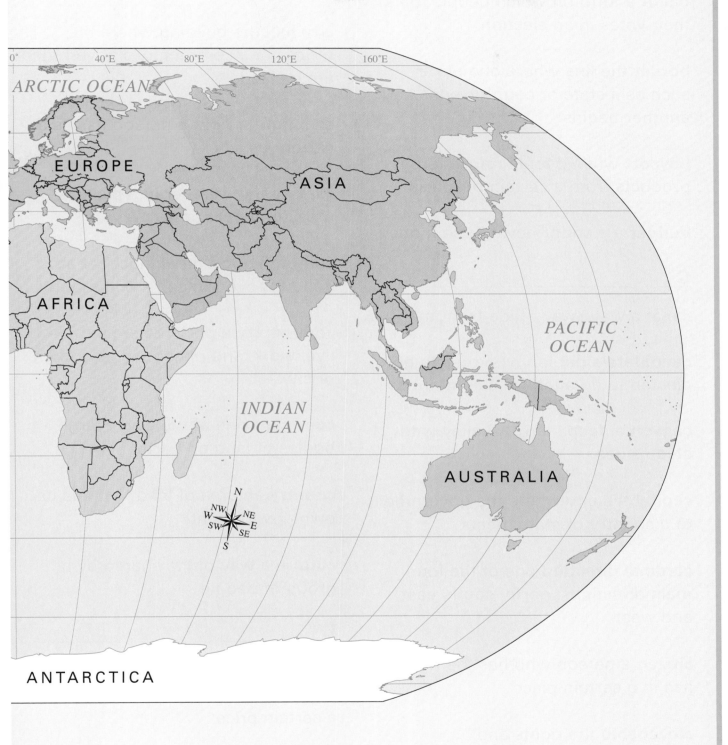

ARCTIC OCEAN

EUROPE

ASIA

AFRICA

PACIFIC
OCEAN

INDIAN
OCEAN

AUSTRALIA

N
NW NE
W E
SW SE
S

ANTARCTICA

40°E   80°E   120°E   160°E

B

ballot a form on which people mark their votes in an election

border the line where one place, such as a state or country, ends and another begins

boycott when people refuse to buy products from a certain business

budget a plan for how to use money

C

canal a waterway made by humans

candidate a person who tries to get elected to do a job for a community

canyon a deep, narrow valley with steep sides

capital the city where the government of a country or state meets

cardinal direction one of the four main directions: north, south, east, and west

citizen a person who has the right to live in a certain place

citizenship the rights and responsibilities of citizens

city a large community with lots of buildings and people

city hall the building where the offices of a community's government are located

civil right a right a person has as a citizen

climate the weather in a place, measured over time

common good the things that are good for everyone in a community

community a place where people live, work, and play, such as a town or city

continent one of the seven large bodies of land on Earth

country an area of land that has its own government

culture a way of life shared by a group of people

D

demand the total amount of a good or service that customers will buy at a certain price

demonstration a gathering of people to show shared feelings or opinions

disabled not being able to do an everyday thing, such as walk, in the same way that most people can

discriminate to treat people unfairly because they belong to a certain group

diverse made up of different groups of people

E

economy all the businesses in a place, such as a community or a country

environment Earth's air, water, soil, and living things

equator the imaginary line that divides Earth into the Northern and Southern hemispheres

F

federal government the national government of the United States

fossil fuel a fuel that comes from the fossils, or remains, of plants or animals

G

geography the study of Earth—its land, water, air, and people

global community all the people, animals, and other living things on Earth

global trade the buying and selling of goods and services between countries around the world

global warming a rise in Earth's temperature over time

goods items that can be bought, sold, and traded, such as food and computers

H

habitat a place where particular animals live

hemisphere half of a sphere

I

immigrant a person who comes from another place to live in a country

J

jury a group of citizens who decide a case in court

L

local government the government of a city, town, county, or other area in the United States that is smaller than a state

M

manufactured made with machines

market a place where buyers and sellers come together

migrant worker someone who moves from place to place to get work

militia an army made up of soldiers who serve during emergencies

N

natural disaster an event in nature, such as an earthquake or flood, that causes great harm

natural resource a useful item that comes from nature, such as wood from trees

nonrenewable resource a natural resource that cannot be made again in a short time

O

ocean one of the four largest bodies of water on Earth

P

patriotism love of your country

peaceful done without hurting others or their property

physical feature a natural feature of Earth's surface, such as a mountain, plain, lake, or river

physical geography the physical features, climate, and natural resources of a place

pollution anything that makes air, water, or soil dirty or unsafe

prime meridian the imaginary line that divides Earth into the Eastern and Western hemispheres

private service a service that is sold by a business

public service a service, such as a public library, that is offered by a community to everyone

public works things such as roads, water pipes, and streetlights that everyone in a community uses

R

region an area with certain features in common

register to sign up to vote

renewable resource a natural resource, such as sunlight, that does not get used up

S

service a task you pay someone to do for you

special-purpose map a map that shows information about a single topic (also called a thematic map)

sphere an object that is shaped like a ball

state one of the 50 main areas with their own governments that make up the United States

state government the government of one of the states of the United States

strike when workers stop working to try to get something they want, such as better pay

suburb a community that grows up on the edge of a city

supply the total amount of a good or service that is available to buy

symbol an object that stands for something else (for example, the Liberty Bell is a symbol of freedom)

T

tax money that people pay to a government

tolerant respectful of other people even if they are different from you

town a community that is smaller than a city

toxic waste poisonous trash or garbage

tradition something that people do together year after year

V

volunteer a person who agrees to do a task without being paid for it

Photographs

Chapter 10

138: Sandy Felsenthal/Corbis
139 TL: Hisham Ibrahim-Photodisc/Getty Images **139 TR:** Owen Franken/Corbis **140:** Roy Ooms/Masterfile
141: Richard Price/Getty Images
142: Owen Franken/Corbis **143:** Cindy Charles/PhotoEdit **144:** Photodisc/Getty Images **145:** North Wind/North Wind Picture Archives **146:** Dave Bartruff/Corbis **147:** Bikestation
148: Paul Barton/Corbis **149:** David Young-Wolff/PhotoEdit **150:** Library of Congress **151 T:** North Wind/North Wind Picture Archives **151 B:** Museum of American History, Smithsonian Institute **152:** Granger Collection, NY **153:** Granger Collection, NY

Chapter 11

156: Owaki/Kulla/Corbis **157:** Owen Franken-RF/Corbis **159:** Peter Cade/Getty Images **160:** Lowell Georgia/Corbis **161:** Dennis MacDonald/PhotoEdit **162:** Frank Siteman/Getty Images **163:** Ron Chapple/Getty Images **164:** Doug Menuez/Getty Images **165:** Bob Rowan Progressive Image/Corbis **167 T:** Bettman/Corbis **167 B:** Photo courtesy of Curt Teich Postcard Archives **168:** Bettmann/Corbis **169 T:** Library of Congress **169 B:** Bettman/Corbis

Chapter 12

172: Tim **173:** Steve Raymer/Corbis **174:** Joseph Sohm-Visions of America/Corbis **175:** Flip Schulke/Corbis **176:** Sergio Dorantes/Corbis **177:** Cory Ryan/Getty Images **178:** Jonathan Nourok/Getty Images **179:** Andy Sachs/Getty Images **180:** Richard Hutchings/Digital Light Source **181:** Richard Hutchings/Digital Light Source **181:** Richard Hutchings/Digital Light Source **182:** Richard Hutchings/Digital Light Source **183:** Richard Hutchings/Digital Light Source

Chapter 13

186: RF/Getty Images **187:** Robert Landau/Corbis **188:** Lori Adamski Peek/Getty Images **189:** Tree Musketeers, El Segundo California **190:** Roy Corral/Corbis **191:** Natalie Fobes/Corbis **192:** Ben Osborne/Getty Images **193:** Karen Kasmauski/Corbis **194:** scottamus/Flickr **195:** Rich Frishman/Getty Images **196:** AP Photo/Paul Vernon **197:** Rob Brimson/Getty Images **198:** Anna Duda/National Renewable Energy Laboratory **199:** Svenja-Foto-zefa/Corbis **200:** IFA Bilderteam/Jupiter Images **201:** Momatiuk - Eastcott/Corbis **201:** Rebecca Reid/NESEA

Chapter 7
88-89: Len Ebert **90**: Len Ebert **92**: Len Ebert **94**: Len Ebert **96**: Len Ebert **98**: Len Ebert **100**: Len Ebert

Chapter 8
108-109: Susan Jaekel

Chapter 9
122-123: Doug Roy

Chapter 10
136-137: Renate Lohmann

Chapter 11
154-155: Len Ebert **166**: Gary Undercuffler

Chapter 12
170-171: Jane McCreary

Chapter 13
184-185: Jane McCreary

Chapter 14
202-203: Doug Roy

Artists represented by Ann Remen-Willis, Artist Representative and Art Manager:

Len Ebert
Dennis Hockerman
Susan Jaekel
Renate Lohmann
Jane McCreary
Doug Roy
DJ Simison
Rosiland Solomon
Gary Undercuffler